Anonymous

The One Hundredth Anniversary of the Paoli Massacre

Proceedings on the Occasion of the Dedication of the Monument - in

Chester County, Pa., September 20, 1877

Anonymous

The One Hundredth Anniversary of the Paoli Massacre
Proceedings on the Occasion of the Dedication of the Monument - in Chester County, Pa., September 20, 1877

ISBN/EAN: 9783337343514

Printed in Europe, USA, Canada, Australia, Japan

Cover: Foto ©Andreas Hilbeck / pixelio.de

More available books at **www.hansebooks.com**

ON THE OCCASION

OF THE

DEDICATION OF THE MONUMENT

ON THE

One Hundredth Anniversary

OF THE

PAOLI MASSACRE,

IN CHESTER COUNTY, PA.,

SEPTEMBER 20, 1877.

WEST CHESTER, PA.
F. S. HICKMAN, STEAM-POWER PRINTER, COR. GAY & CHURCH STS.
1877.

THE MASSACRE AT PAOLI.

On the Fourth of July, 1817, the Republican Artillerists of Chester County, at the instance of the late Dr. William Darlington, resolved to enclose in a durable manner, the graves of the brave men who perished in the massacre near the Paoli on the twentieth of September, 1777, and also to erect a suitable monument to their memory. The work was proceeded with, the graves enclosed with a substantial stone wall, and a handsome marble monument about nine feet in height, appropriately inscribed, was procured and erected in the centre of the enclosure.

On the twentieth of September, 1817—the fortieth anniversary of the massacre—the monument was dedicated with appropriate military honors. A full account of the proceedings on the occasion will be found in the appendix. The surrounding grounds, containing about twenty-three acres, were subsequently conveyed to the military organizations of Chester and Delaware counties, to be held in trust for a parade ground. They are situated in Willistown township, Chester county, about half-a-mile from the junction of the West Chester and Pennsylvania railroads, at Malvern station.

The monument thus erected having, in the lapse of years, become very much injured and defaced, and being no longer a fitting memorial to the heroic dead, steps were taken to procure the erection of a new one, and at a meeting held on the grounds on July 4th, 1875, composed of the military of the district, of the organization known as the Centennial Minute Men of Chester County, and of private citizens, the project as-

(3)

sumed a definite shape.   After an oration by Major A. C. Fulton, of West Chester, the following paper was read by Dr. J. B. Wood :

" On the twentieth of September next, ninety-eight years will have passed by since a portion of the veteran band engaged in our struggle for independence, encamped here for the night—resting from the fatigue of the battle at Brandywine, which took place only a few days before.   While thus encamped, a portion of troops engaged in the army of the British crown suddenly surprised them, and the dreadful massacre, unparalleled by savage or barbaric precedents, which is familiar to you all, took place on this spot, and the monument now before you (partially destroyed by vandal hands) has been erected in memory of those who laid down their lives in order that we should enjoy the blessing of a free government such as the world had never seen.

We have met to commemorate on this spot one of the natal days of the nation, and to devise ways and means to put this monument and these grounds in proper repair, and to take such steps as will tend to their preservation in the future.

I am aware that something has already been done by the military of this district to consummate so desirable a purpose, but the response to their efforts has been but a feeble one.

They want aid, and I propose that we each give ten dollars for this purpose, which will not be more than our military friends lose annually in order to be prepared to defend our firesides in time of need, and I am sure that every citizen of this community will feel a pride in having contributed for so desirable a purpose.

To our " Minute Men " I now appeal. . We are engaged to commemorate all the prominent events in our struggle for independence, and it is highly important that proper arrangements shall now be inaugurated for September 1877, on this spot, and the first thing to be done will be the fitting up of this monument and the surrounding grounds.''

The appeal thus made was nobly responded to, and a considerable sum subscribed on the spot.

The project was taken in charge by a committee of the military of the District, who, in consequence of the great interest taken by Dr. Wood, honored him with the position of Chairman. This committee consisted of Dr. J. B. Wood, Col. Alfred Rupert, Col. F. A. Tencate, Col. Daniel P. Moore, Major B. F.

Bean, Major A. C. Fulton, and Captains John Denithorne, James E. McFarlan, Wilson M. Matlack and Robert T. Cornwell.

The necessary funds were collected, the monument constructed and placed in position, an iron railing placed around the mound, the parade grounds put in complete order, and the necessary arrangements made for the dedication of the monument on the twentieth of September, 1877—the one hundredth anniversary of the massacre. In the performance of this labor, especial credit is due to Dr. Wood, who originated the project, and through whose indefatigable and untiring exertions the necessary funds were raised,* and the affair brought to a successful termination, and the thanks of all true patriots should be accorded to him for his unselfish labor of love.

The monument is of Quincy granite, twenty-two feet and a-half in height, chaste and rich and impressive in its simplicity. A square pedestal of rugged granite supports a sub-base of similar material but smaller proportions ; on this rests the die with its inscriptions ; from which springs upward a plain granite shaft, the whole making a well proportioned obelisk. On the west face of the shaft is cut in bold letters the word PAOLI, while the polished die bears the following inscriptions :

WEST SIDE.

Sacred
to the memory of the
PATRIOTS
who on this spot
fell a sacrifice to
British barbarity
during the struggle for
AMERICAN INDEPENDENCE,
on the night of the
20th of September, 1777.

NORTH SIDE.

THE ATROCIOUS MASSACRE
which this stone commemorates
was perpetrated
by British troops
under the immediate command
of
MAJOR GENERAL GREY.

*To Luke Bemis, Esq., of Massachusetts, Superintendent of the Government Paper Mills at Glen Mills, Pa., credit is due for valuable assistance.

SOUTH SIDE.

Here repose
the remains of fifty-three
AMERICAN SOLDIERS,
who were the
victims of cold-blooded cruelty
in the well known
"MASSACRE AT THE PAOLI,"
while under the command
of
GENERAL ANTHONY WAYNE,
an officer
whose military conduct,
bravery and humanity,
were equally conspicuous
throughout the
REVOLUTIONARY WAR.

EAST SIDE.

Erected by the citizens of
Chester and Delaware counties,
September 20, 1877, being
THE CENTENNIAL ANNIVERSARY
of the Paoli Massacre.

The other inscriptions on this monument are
copied from
the memorial stone
formerly standing here,
which was erected by
the Republican Artillerists,
and other citizens of
Chester County,
September 20, 1817.

These inscriptions, (except that on the east side) taken from the old monument, were written by Dr. William Darlington, who was the master spirit on the occasion of its erection in 1817.

The monument is built upon a mound of about three feet, giving it an elevation of twenty-five feet. On the south end of the mound stands the old monument, erected in 1817, which is preserved as a relic of the past. It is nine feet in height, has a base of blue marble and pedestal of white marble, upon which are the inscriptions as above mentioned. The stone wall was removed, and the whole plot is surrounded by a wrought iron picket fence, five feet high.

When the corner stone of the new monument was laid, a copper box was placed at its base, containing the following articles :

1. Original subscription list, dated July 4th, 1875, with name of projector of monument and the subscriptions obtained on that day.

2. Address on Monument project to the citizens of Chester county.

3. List of contributors.

4. Specifications and contract.

5. Officers of the day.

6. Large handbill of dedication ceremonies.

7. Portrait of Gen. Anthony Wayne.

8. Chester and Delaware county newspapers.

9. Names of President and Vice President of the United States.

10. Name of the Governor of Pennsylvania.

11. Names of County officers, with their signatures.

12. Confederate money : $50, $20, $5, $1.

13. Specimens of Colonial and Continental money.

14. Likenesses of President and Vice President of United States.

15. Ticket of admission to the counting of the Electoral vote, 1877, House of Representatives, signed by T. W. Ferry, President of Senate, and Samuel J. Randall, Speaker of House.

16. Silver coins, as follows: Trade dollar, ordinary dollar, half dollar, quarter dollar, dime and two three cent pieces; five cent nickel, two cent piece, one cent piece, old copper penny, and half-penny, copper.

The twentieth of September, 1877, was a day which will long live in the annals of Chester county. The sky was unclouded, and the balmy air seemed to invite the people to turn out in holiday garb and greet each other upon the historic field of Paoli. At an early hour they began to gather from all directions, in carriages, on horseback and on foot ; military and civic processions paraded into the grounds to the music of bands and drum corps, and the numerous trains on the West Chester and Pennsylvania railroads added their quota to the moving tide of humanity, until as the hour approached for the commencement of the exercises, the grounds seemed to be literally covered with people. There was such an assemblage as had never before convened on the soil of Chester county. The number present was variously estimated at from eight to ten thousand persons.

The military and civic display was under the charge of Col.
Alfred Rupert as Chief Marshal, who had as Aids, Col. H. H.
Gilkyson, Phœnixville ; Major Percy R. Hoskins, West Goshen ;
Major M. M. Ellis, Phœnixville ; Major Rob't G. Woodside, Ox-
ford ; Charles W. Roberts, East Goshen ; Lewis H. Evans, Up-
per Uwchlan ; Charles S. Bradford, Jr., West Chester ; B. F.
Davis, Easttown ; Harry S. Hickman, Thornbury ; Joseph
James, West Chester ; J. Havard Downing, West Whiteland ;
George R. Hoopes, West Chester ; Jacob P. Ringwalt, Down-
ingtown ; George Little, East Bradford ; Alan Hartshorne, West
Chester ; H. B. Thompson, Willistown ; Abram Deery, West
Pikeland ; Samuel Fetters, East Whiteland ; Harry Wells, Tredyffrin, and Zimmerman Colehower, Charlestown. The com-
mittee of arrangements consisted of Dr. J. B. Wood, Col. Alfred
Rupert, Major A. C. Fulton, Captain Robert T. Cornwell, and
Captain James E. McFarlan.   John A. Groff, Esq., President of
the "Centennial Minute Men," was chairman of a committee
on delegations from the various townships.

Governor John F. Hartranft, who had been invited to honor
the occasion with his presence, arrived at the Paoli station, on
the Pennsylvania railroad, about nine o'clock, accompanied by
his military staff, composed of Gen. James W. Latta, Adjutant
General of the State, Gen. L. W. Read, Gen. George F. Smith,
Col. D. S. Hassinger, Col. John Schall, Col. C. S. Greene, Col.
R. R. Campion ; and Major L. D. Baugh, of Gen. Brinton's
staff ; Hon. John B. Linn, Deputy Secretary of the Common-
wealth, and Captain A. L. Snowden of the First City Troop, and
were received by a committee, and by the Washington Troop,
commanded by Captain Matlack, which had been detailed for
the occasion. The whole party then entered carriages, and
under the escort of the Troop, accompanied by Gen. John
R. Dobson and staff, and by a large number of other invited
guests, proceeded to the residence of Captain William Wayne,
where a bountiful breakfast had been provided.

Capt. Wayne, who is a lineal descendant of General Anthony
Wayne, received and greeted his visitors with a cordiality that
at once made them feel welcome. He occupies the old mansion in which his distinguished ancestor resided, and which is lo-
cated about one mile from the Paoli station. It is a spacious

stone structure with large, airy rooms, such as only the wealthy land owners in olden times could occupy. The room to the right of the main hall possesses the greatest interest, and the visitor is at once impressed with the ancient character of the surroundings. Here is the antique furniture which occupied the room when the General was living; the very same carpet—Brussels—is on the floor, upon which he trod, and the same lambrequins and decorations over the windows. There is the old-fashioned open fire-place, with its andirons, fender, and shovel and tongs. On the mantel are the silver snuffers

WAYNE MANSION.

and tray; above them is a portrait of Gen. Wayne in uniform; and across that are placed his sword and two famous horse-pistols that officers carried in their holsters in olden times.

In this room had been Washington and the other Generals, whose names were made famous by their deeds of heroism during the Revolution. Here Lafayette was received upon his return to this country after the Revolution; and there hang the same window-curtains that were especially provided for that occasion. The Captain exhibited to his guests the military coat worn by Gen. Wayne, with gilt buttons and buff facing, and presenting a much more showy appearance than the military coats of the present day; he also exhibited the watch worn by the General, and a number of other relics of great historical interest.

PAOLI MASSACRE.

After breakfast, the whole party, preceded by the Washington Troop, repaired to the monument grounds, and were met at the western entrance by Col. Alfred Rupert, the Chief Marshal of the day, and his aids, and as the procession moved across the field, the military organizations were drawn in line to receive the Governor, and presented an imposing sight. A Governor's salute of seventeen guns was fired by the Griffen Battery.

At twelve o'clock the meeting, which was held in the grove immediately west of and near the monument, was organized by Dr. Wood, who named the following officers:

President,
HON. WASHINGTON TOWNSEND.

Vice Presidents,

Capt. Wm. Wayne,	Dr. J. L. Forwood,
John D. Evans,	Charles D. Manley, Esq.,
Dr. John R. Hoskins,	David Ruth, Esq.,
Jesse Matlack,	Tryon Lewis,
Abraham Fetters, Jr.,	Dr. Geo. Smith,
Isaac W. Vanleer,	P. Frazer Smith, Esq.,
Gen. Geo. Hartman,	David Ramsay,
Dr. Jacob Rickabaugh,	John Irey,
Chandler Phillips,	Matthew Barker,
Col. F. B. Speakman,	Hon. Jesse C. Dickey,
John McWilliams,	Capt. Samuel Holman,
Evans Rogers,	J. Lacey Darlington,
Robert E. Monaghan, Esq.,	Harmon Bond,
Col. N. M. Ellis,	Wm. T. Shafer,
John O. K. Robarts,	Hon. John M. Broomall,
John P. Thornbury,	Rob't L. McClellan,
Edwin Otley,	Nimrod Strickland,
Hon. William Ward,	Wellington Hickman,
James M. Willcox,	W. Cooper Talley.

Secretaries,

Maj. A. C. Fulton,	Barton D. Evans,
R. Jones Monaghan,	W. I. Kauffman,
W. W. Thomson,	Henry L. Brinton,
Thos. V. Cooper,	John Miller,
Wm. W. Polk,	Edward B. Moore,
Wm. H. Hodgson,	Ezra Evans,

Vosburg Schaeffer.

The exercises were then conducted in the following order:

1. Delivery of monument by Mr. VanGunden, on behalf of Messrs. VanGunden, Young and Drumm of Philadelphia, the contractors, to the Committee.

2. Reception of the same on behalf of the Committee by Captain Robert T. Cornwell.

3. Presentation of Monument by Dr. Wood on behalf of the Committee to the President, for dedication.

4. Address of Hon. Washington Townsend at dedication.

5. Unveiling of monument by Dr. Wood.

6. National salute of thirty-eight guns by Griffin Battery.

7. Prayer by Rev. Joseph S. Evans.

8. Historical address by J. Smith Futhey, Esq.

9. Oration by Hon. Wayne MacVeagh.

10. Benediction by Rev. Mr. Elliott.

At the conclusion of the foregoing programme, the military and citizens formed in line, and to the solemn music of the bands and the low roll of the muffled drums, marched slowly around the monument. It was a very impressive ceremony.

The order of march was as follows :

General John R. Dobson and Staff.
Col. Alfred Rupert and Aids.

Washington Troop, of Glenloch, Chester county,
Capt. Wilson M. Matlack.

Griffen Battery, of Phœnixville and West Chester,
Capt. John Denithorne.

11th Regt. Pa. National Guards Band of Phœnixville, 15 pieces,
Capt. B. Frank Dunhower.

Wayne Fencibles, Co. "I," 11th Regt. N. G. Pa.,
Capt. Robert T. Cornwell.

West Chester Greys, Co. "E," 11th Regt. N. G. Pa., with
drum corps, Lieut. Henry M. Worth commanding.

Cooper Rifles of Media, Co. "G," 11th Regt. N. G. Pa.,
Captain John W. Russell

Wheatly Cadets of Phœnixville, Co. "D," 11th Regt.
N. G. Pa., Captain Samuel Wilson.

Reeves Rifles of Phœnixville, Co. "A," 11th Regt.
N. G. Pa., Capt. Samuel Gilbert.

Coatesville Guards, Co. "C," 11th Regt. N. G. Pa.,
Captain Caleb Brown.

Delaney Guards (col.) Independent, of West Chester,
Captain Levi M. Hood.

West Chester Pioneer Corps, Captain
J. Lacey Darlington, Jr.

Coatesville Pioneer Corps.

Chester Springs Soldiers' Orphans' School, 62 boys, clad
in blue uniforms.

Valley Forge Cornet Band, 16 pieces.

Township Delegations followed, representing, among others,
Tredyffrin, Uwchlan, Pikeland, Schuylkill, Charlestown and Easttown, the latter carrying a banner
bearing the words—"Easttown, the home
of General Wayne."

This ended the formal exercises of the day, the vast assemblage slowly departed, and when the shades of evening fell
over the scene, there was nothing left but the old monument
and the new, over the dust of the dead.

Altogether, it was an event long to be remembered, and
during the whole day there occurred nothing to mar any feature of the occasion.

DELIVERY OF MONUMENT BY MR. VANGUNDEN, ON BEHALF OF THE CON-
TRACTORS FOR ITS ERECTION, TO THE COMMITTEE.

Gentlemen of the Paoli Monument Committee :—On the 14th
day of March of this year, Dr. J. B. Wood, Col. Alfred Rupert,
Maj. A. C. Fulton, and Capt. R. T. Cornwell, on behalf of Committee, contracted with us for the construction of this monument.

We feel ourselves doubly honored in being chosen by you
for the performance of this work, for we have had not only the
artist's pleasure, but as American citizens, in common with you,
we have felt gratified in being permitted—though in an humble
way—to perpetuate the memory of those Revolutionary Patriots, who, betrayed by another *Arnold*, were on the 20th day
of September, 1777—one hundred years ago to-day—massacred by our enemies.

We have, with conscious integrity, devoted our best skill to
the execution of the task confided to us.

And now, gentlemen, with thanks to you for your uniform
courtesy and kindness, I place in your custody the results of our
united labors, and may the memory of your patriotic devotion to-
day, and the deeds of the noble dead whose ashes sleep beneath
this monument, be preserved in the annals of a grateful country
until the end of time.

RECEPTION OF MONUMENT ON BEHALF OF THE COMMITTEE, BY CAPT.
ROBERT T. CORNWELL.

Messrs. VanGunden, Young & Drumm—

GENTLEMEN :—I have been designated as one of the members

of the Committee on Monument to here publicly receive the work at your hands; and in doing so I am instructed to say that we are highly gratified with the manner in which it has been performed. You have done all, and more than all, that your contract with us required. You have given us, without extra charge, a granite superior in hardness, tenacity and durability, as well as in its freedom from liability to discoloration, though you informed us, when you submitted your proposal and accepted the contract, that if we determined upon granite of the character used, we must pay a considerable addition to the contract price. That the large amount of engraving upon the monument might be rendered thoroughly legible and distinct, you have at your own expense and volition subjected the whole die to a beautiful polish. There are other minor additions that you have made a free will offering to the work. We are satisfied, sirs, that from first to last, you have been solely prompted by a desire to erect a monument upon these grounds that should be at once creditable to yourselves and to its projectors, and a fitting memorial through which the brave Revolutionary patriots who perished here might speak to future generations. The result is the beautiful and durable column we see before us.

WE ACCEPT IT, without a word of adverse criticism, and with its price we tender you the grateful acknowledgments of the Committee, and of the citizens of Chester and Delaware counties who have contributed to its erection.

PRESENTATION OF MONUMENT BY DR. WOOD, CHAIRMAN OF THE COMMITTEE, TO THE PRESIDENT, FOR DEDICATION.

Mr. President :—On behalf of the Committee of the Minute Men, and the Committee of the Military of Chester and Delaware Counties, I respectfully report that in July, 1875, they commenced the work of raising money for a new monument to take the place of the one heretofore erected, which is mutilated and defaced.

In that effort they were successful, and so reported to the military officers having charge of these grounds.

Whereupon the said officers after due notice given, appointed the undersigned, in connection with the Staff Officers of the

11th Regiment, and the Captains of the several companies thereof in Chester and Delaware Counties, a Committee to take the necessary steps to have the said monument erected against the occurrence of the centennial anniversary of the massacre.

The said Committee therefore respectfully report that they contracted with Messrs. VanGunden, Young & Drumm, of the city of Philadelphia, for the erection of the same, and the result is the beautiful shaft of granite before you about to be unveiled, and which the Committee now place in your hands for the purpose of dedication.

Respectfully submitted,

J. B. Wood, *Chairman of Committee.*

ADDRESS OF HON. WASHINGTON TOWNSEND, THE PRESIDENT, AT DEDICATION.

Mr. Chairman :—I receive at your hands with much gratification the handsome monument which we will unveil to-day, and whose existence is due to the energetic labors of the Committees of Minute Men and the Military, aided by the citizens at large.

I proceed to its dedication :

Officers and Soldiers, Friends and Fellow Countrymen—

We are here to-day in the discharge of a patriotic duty. We are here to express our grateful remembrance of the men who, in the revolution, toiled and struggled through a long, tedious and exhausting war, to assert and establish the right of self-government, and to plant on this continent the seeds of civil and religious liberty.

Our chief object, however, on this occasion, is to preserve the memory of the Revolutionary soldiers who, on this spot, gave up their lives while in the endeavor to secure the inestimable privileges which we now enjoy.

It is a century ago to-day since a little band of American soldiers, retreating from the disastrous and bloody field of Brandywine, where they had resolutely fought, were encamped where we now stand.

With sentinels posted at night and the usual military precautions taken, they dreamed not of danger, but deemed themselves secure. A traitor's hand, however, pointed out to the enemy the secret pathways to their camp; a stealthy march enabled the foe to reach their position, and in the darkness of midnight fifty-three of them fell ruthlessly slain, victims of British barbarity.

Just sixty years ago the Republican Artillerists of Chester County, aided by other patriotic citizens, a few of whom still survive and are with us to-day, wishing to perpetuate the remembrance of their heroism and their sufferings, erected here a handsome marble monument to their memory.

The destroying hand of time, and the vandalism of relic hunters have mutilated that monument, have curtailed its proportions and destroyed its beauty.

Earnest and patriotic men now before and around me, from the military ranks and the walks of civil life, have determined that so far as they can prevent it, neither time nor vandalism shall hinder from keeping fresh in the hearts and the minds of the people the memory of the patriot soldiers who fell here.

To secure that end, they have erected a grander and more enduring memorial stone of substantial material, beautiful in form, design and proportion, and admirable in execution, on whose sides will be found engraven deep the history of that disastrous night.

It will serve, it is hoped, for many generations to come, as an altar around which lovers of their country will annually assemble to render their tribute of admiration for the patriots of that day; it shall serve as a place where men shall teach lessons of patriotism to their children, and where they shall keep alive as well, the remembrance of the services and sacrifices of revolutionary heroes.

Around such altars the people of monarchies gather to celebrate the exploits of military leaders, and the deeds of kings whose victories have tended to rivet the chains of despotism upon the people, but ours will be the grateful duty to celebrate upon this consecrated ground the virtues and services of those, more meritorious, who struggled to secure civil and religious liberty to American citizens.

Time and the seasons may, however, wear the inscriptions on this monument away; the memorial stone itself, like most earthly things, may crumble into dust, but however that may

be, a grateful people will never forget the martyrdom of the
soldiers of the revolution, who in this field were slain, defending the holy cause of liberty, so long as the word " Paoli " shall
be heard amongst men, and the name of Wayne shall be inscribed on the pages of our revolutionary history.

In the name and on behalf of the military and the people, I
accept from the Committee, whose generous and untiring labors
have erected it, this magnificent monument ; I deliver it and
entrust it to their care and protection, and in their presence,
cheered with the presence of descendants now around me, of
Wayne, Frazer and Lacey, and other revolutionary heroes, on
this Centennial anniversary of the Paoli massacre I dedicate it
and consecrate it to the memory of the patriots who fell upon
this field, and to the memory of their gallant and distinguished
commander, General Anthony Wayne.

At the conclusion of Mr. Townsend's address, the monument was unveiled by Dr. Wood, revealing the neat proportions of the appropriate testimonial to the fallen heroes.

The Griffen Battery then fired a national salute of thirty-
eight guns, and the graceful and well disciplined evolutions of
the men enlisted marked attention.

PRAYER BY REV. JOSEPH S. EVANS.

Almighty and ever blessed God : the Father of our Lord
Jesus Christ, and the Father of all who come to Thee in His
name ; in whose hand are the destinies of individuals, as well
as the destinies of the nations of the earth ! Before Thee we
humbly bow at this time to express the gratitude of our hearts
for the many blessings we enjoy at Thy hand.   .

As it did please Thee, in thine all-wise Providence, that our
forefathers should suffer and die as martyrs to the great cause
of liberty, we thank Thee that we are permitted to stand upon
this sacred spot, hallowed to our memories by the baptism of
their blood, in the rich enjoyment of the fruits of their sacrifice.

We thank Thee for our Nation's prosperity and greatness.
We thank Thee for the glorious banner of freedom, under
whose folds we this day gather—the proud emblem of a nation's
greatness, and universal liberty wherever its beautiful stars

and stripes are unfurled. God of mercy, perpetuate our prosperity and our freedom.

And now we crave Thy blessing upon us as we thus come together to reiterate, by these exercises, and the unveiling of this monument, our grateful remembrance of the heroic deeds of our martyred dead. Bless us while here; bless us as we go hence. And now as we so gratefully remember the human sacrifice of those who sleep beneath this sod, O may we remember and trust in that greater, richer sacrifice, the precious blood of thy dear son, who gave Himself as our substitute, and suffered and died in our stead, that whosoever trusteth in him should not perish, but have everlasting life and blessing through faith in His name. And to Father, Son and Holy Spirit, will we ascribe all glory and praise, now and evermore. Amen!

HISTORICAL ADDRESS OF J. SMITH FUTHEY.

For three-quarters of a century after the establishment by William Penn of his peaceful province of Pennsylvania, that portion of his colony known as the county of Chester enjoyed a singular immunity from strife and bloodshed. The time arrived, however, when the soil of our goodly county was to be pressed by the foot of the invader, and our citizens, theretofore exempt from the calamities of war, were to see their fields crossed by hostile armies and made the theatre of military operations, while many of them, throwing aside the implements of husbandry, and forgetting for a time the arts and employments of peace, were to mingle in the general strife.

Early in the Revolutionary contest, Chester County became the scene of military operations. Our people deeply participated in the indignation excited throughout the colonies by the oppressive and arbitrary measures of the British Government, and when the call to arms was made, they responded with alacrity, and contributed a full proportion of men for the service, and evinced a spirit scarcely to be expected among a people so generally opposed in principle to the practice of war. But a high enthusiasm at that time prevailed for the cause of the insulted and endangered liberties of our country, animating all ranks and classes, and inciting them to resist by

arms the progress of usurpation, so that few, not absolutely
restrained by scruples of conscience, felt disposed to disregard
the call when their aid was required.

It is to be remembered also, that while the members of the
Society of Friends—who in principle were opposed to war—
largely preponderated in the eastern and central portions of
the county, the southern, western, and northwestern portions
thereof were principally inhabited by that sturdy and independent race known as the Scotch-Irish—a race, who in the
maintenance of civil and religious liberty and of inflexible
resistance to all usurpation in church and state, were not sur-
passed by any class of settlers in the American Colonies. Many
of these people had emigrated to America, in consequence of
the oppression of the large landed proprietors, shortly before the
breaking out of the Revolutionary war; and, leaving the Old
World in such a temper, they became a powerful contribution
to the cause of liberty, and to the separation of the colonies
from the mother country. To show the extent to which they
engaged in the service, it may be stated that in the campaign
of 1777, every able-bodied man in the large Presbyterian
congregation of Brandywine Manor, in Chester County, was
in the army, and the gathering of the harvest and putting in
of the fall crops were performed by the old men, women, and
children. It was perhaps the only race of all that settled in
the western world that never produced one tory. The nearest
approach to one was a man who was brought before a church
session, and tried upon the charge that he was "suspected of
not being sincere in his professions of his attachment to the
cause of the revolution." The Scotch-Irish were a race who
emphatically feared not the face of man, and who put their
trust in God *and their rifles.*

The descendants of the Welsh and the Swedes were also
numerous in this county—especially in the eastern and some
of the northern townships—and contributed largely to swell the
number of those who were ready at the bugle's call, to buckle
on their armor with alacrity, and fight for liberty.

To John Morton, a citizen of Chester, now Delaware County,
a member of the Continental Congress, belongs the high honor

of having voted for the Declaration of Independence, and thus, with Franklin and Wilson, who also voted in its favor, secured the voice of Pennsylvania.

The first military force raised in Chester County was a regiment of volunteers, of which the gallant Anthony Wayne, then a farmer, residing about two miles from this spot, was appointed Colonel, and Richard Thomas, Lieutenant-Colonel. Col. Wayne soon afterwards joined the regular army, and the command devolved upon Col. Thomas. This regiment was raised as early as September, 1775. A second regiment was raised soon after the first had been formed, and officered principally by inhabitants of Chester County. Subsequently to this and throughout the war, this county contributed its full quota to fill up the armies of the republic.

It was a leading object of the British, early in the war, to occupy Philadelphia, and the campaign of 1777 was devoted by Sir William Howe and the forces under his command to that purpose. The importance of this place in a military point of view has been questioned on both sides, and Washington and Howe have both been censured for their pertinacity. Philadelphia was at that time the largest city in the revolted provinces : it was the seat of the Continental Congress, and the centre of the colonies. Although commanding easy access to the sea, it was capable of being readily protected from the approach of a hostile fleet, and it lay in the heart of an open, extended country, rich, comparatively populous, and, so far, but little disturbed by the war. It was, in a sense regarded as the capital of the new-born nation, and the moral influence resulting from its occupation by Congress was great, and it was deemed that an important point would be gained by its conquest. While the seat of Congress was secure, men were led to mock at the army which could not penetrate to the head-quarters of the infant nation. Another reason was the fact that the region around Philadelphia was, owing to its position, and the peaceful disposition of much of its population, less affected by the yoke of Britain, and less influenced by the enthusiasm of the other colonies, after the first excitement had subsided. In the possession of the British, this dis-

affection to the cause of the revolution, it was thought by
them, would tend to strengthen their hold upon the country.

With this end in view, the British fleet under Lord Howe, bearing a land force eighteen thousand strong, left New York in July,
1777, with the intention of approaching Philadelphia by way of
the Delaware River. When about to enter it, however, the
British commander was informed that the Americans had placed
obstructions in the channel, and he therefore proceeded to the
Chesapeake. up which he sailed, and on the 25th of August landed
his forces at what was known as Turkey Point. near the head
of the bay, with the view of proceeding eastward towards
Philadelphia.[1]

The departure of the British fleet from New York was the
signal for the march of the American troops to the southward. Washington was in some perplexity, being uncertain
as to its objects, but directed the concentration of the army on
the Neshaminy. in Bucks County, Pennsylvania, so as to meet
the enemy should he attempt to approach Philadelphia, or to
proceed northward should the New England States prove to be
Howe's destination. As soon, however, as Washington was
informed that the fleet was off the Capes of the Chesapeake, he
turned his attention in that direction. On the 23d of August,
the Americans left their encampment and marched down the
Old York Road to Germantown where they spent the night.
The next day they passed through Philadelphia, Washington
with Lafayette[2] at his side riding at the head of the column.
On the 25th, the day the British landed at the Head of Elk.
they marched to Wilmington, and encamped on Red Clay Creek,
a few miles below that place. Their whole effective force fit
for duty was about eleven thousand men.

Washington made immediate preparations to oppose the
march of the enemy. From the first movements in advance

[1] Howe, in his "narrative." says that, upon finding it would be "extremely
hazardous" to attempt to proceed up the Delaware, he "agreed with the Admiral
to go up Chesapeake Bay. a plan which had been preconcerted in the event of a
landing in the Delaware proving, upon our arrival there, ineligible," which
movement is said to have been the treasonable suggestion of Charles Lee. See
Treason of Charles Lee, by Geo. H. Moore, N. Y., 1860.

[2] Lafayette first entered the army while it lay on the banks of the Neshaminy.

from the Head of Elk, active skirmishing, sometimes of considerable bodies, took place, in which the Americans made a number of prisoners. On the 3d of September a severe though brief encounter occurred at Iron Hill, Pencader Hundred, Delaware, between a division of the British under Cornwallis and Knyphausen, and a body of Americans under the command of Gen. Maxwell. On the 8th the American army took its position behind Red Clay Creek, the left resting upon Newport, and the right extending a considerable distance up the creek to Hockesson. Here a battle was anticipated. Washington, however, from the movements of the enemy, saw that their object was to turn his right, cross the Brandywine, and cut off his communication with Philadelphia, which, if successfully carried out in the position which he then occupied, would have hemmed him in between the British army and their fleet, where he must have been overpowered, or compelled to fight his way out under every disadvantage. He accordingly, after reconnoitering the enemy, withdrew to Chads' Ford, on the Brandywine, where he arrived on the 9th of September, and took up his position on the east side of the stream, and entrenched himself on the high ground immediately north of the present Chads' Ford Hotel. Maxwell's light infantry occupied the advanced posts, and during the night of the 10th threw up defences on the west side, at the approaches to the ford. At this spot, in the beautiful valley of Chester County's classic stream, Washington resolved to take his stand, and do battle in defence of the City of Brotherly Love.[1]

[1] The charms of the scenery of Chester County have found frequent expression in poetry as well as in prose; but nowhere more suitably, or with more spirit, than in the language of her own son, the late T. Buchanan Read. The reproduction of the following lines, from his "Wagoner of the Alleghanies," is particularly appropriate at this time.

The hour was loud, but louder still
  Anon the rage of battle roared
Its wild and murderous will;
  From Jefferis down to Wistar's ford,
  From Jones to Chads, the cannon poured,
While thundered Osborne Hill.
Oh, ne'er before fled holy calm
  From out its sainted house of prayer
  So frighted through the trembling air
As from that shrine of Birmingham!

On the evening of the 9th of September the British army entered Chester County in two divisions, one of which, under Gen. Knyphausen, encamped at New Garden and Kennet Square, and the other, under Cornwallis, a short distance below Hockesson Meeting House. Early next day they united at Kennet Square, whence in the evening the forces under Knyphausen advanced towards Welsh's tavern, now known as the Anvil, probably for the convenience of water, and those under Cornwallis remained encamped on the hills north and west of Kennet Square.

On the morning of the 11th the army divided into two columns—one division, under Knyphausen, marching directly through Kennet and Pennsbury Townships to Chads' Ford, by the Philadelphia road; and the other, under Cornwallis, and accompanied by Sir William Howe, taking a circuitous route, traversing portions of the townships of Kennet, East Marlborough, Newlin, West Bradford, East Bradford, and Birmingham, crossing the west branch of the Brandywine at Trimble's Ford, a short distance south of Marshalton, and the east branch mainly at Jefferis' Ford, and approaching Birmingham Meeting House from the north: the object of these movements being to hem the Americans in between the two forces, and thus make them an easy prey.

Oft through the opening cloud we scanned
The shouting leaders, sword in hand,
  Directing the tumultuous scene;
There galloped Maxwell, gallant Bland,
  The Poet-warrior, while between,
Ringing o'er all his loud command,
  Dashed the intrepid Greene.

Here Sullivan in fury trooped,
There Weedon like an eagle swooped,
With Muhlenberg—where they were grouped
  The invader dearly earned his gains;
And (where the mad should only be,
  The fiercest champion of the free)
  The loudest trumpet-call was Wayne's:
While in a gale of battle-glee,
  With rapid sword and pistol dealing
  The blows which set the foeman reeling,
Sped "Light-horse Harry Lee."

The column under Cornwallis set out about daybreak, and
that under Knyphausen about nine o'clock. A very dense
and heavy fog continued until a late hour. The column under Knyphausen skirmished with the advanced parties of the
American army sent forward to harass the march of the
British troops. Maxwell's corps, which occupied the hills
west of the Brandywine, was driven across the stream after a
severe engagement, and joined the main body of the American army, which was ranged in order of battle, awaiting the
attack of the enemy. Several detachments of the Americans
subsequently recrossed the creek and assailed the British,
who were laboring to throw up entrenchments and plant bat-
teries. A footing having been secured on the western bank,
Gen. Maxwell returned in force, and a warm conflict ensued ;
the Americans driving the enemy from the ground. The
sharpness of the skirmish soon drew upon them overwhelm-
ing numbers, and the Americans were again repulsed. Knyphausen paraded on the heights, reconnoitering the American
army, and by various movements appeared to be making dispositions to force a passage of the stream, and every moment
the attempt was expected to be made.

Gen. Cornwallis, with the larger division of the British
army, under the cover of the hills and forests, and aided by
the fog, proceeded in the circuitous route a considerable distance unobserved, and must have reached the hills south of
Trimble's Ford about the time that Knyphausen moved from
his position east of Kennet Square. Some cannons were discharged at this point (and cannon-balls have been found in
the vicinity) for which it is difficult to account, unless they
were designed to notify Knyphausen that they had gained a
midway position, or to direct him to march to the Ford.

Gen. Sullivan, who commanded the right wing of the American army, had received instructions to guard the fords as
high up as Buffington's—now Shaw's—just above the forks
of the Brandywine, and scouting parties were sent out in
various directions to watch the movements of the enemy.
About one o'clock intelligence was brought that the enemy's
left wing was about crossing the Brandywine above its forks,

and Col. Bland sent word to Washington that a large force
was seen advancing up the road towards Trimble's Ford, and
this was confirmed by a note from Col. Ross who was in their
rear, and who estimated the force that he had seen at not less
than five thousand.   Washington, on receiving this intelligence
of a large division being so far separated from the army at
Chads' Ford, formed the design of detaching Sullivan and
Lord Stirling to engage the column conducted by Cornwallis,
should he attempt to cross the stream, while he in person
should cross over with the residue of the troops and attack
the forces under Knyphausen.

In pursuance of this determination, Sterling was despatched
with a considerable force to occupy the high ground in the
vicinity of Birmingham Meeting House, while other necessary

BIRMINGHAM MEETING HOUSE.

dispositions were made upon the left.   At the critical moment
when the plan was about to be executed, counter-intelligence
was received, inducing the opinion that the movement of
Cornwallis was merely a feint, and that after making demon-
strations of crossing the Brandywine above its forks, he must
actually have marched down the right bank of the stream,
and was about to re-unite his column with that of Knyphausen.   This opinion was confirmed by the report of a number
of light horse that had been sent to reconnoitre.

While Washington was in a state of painful uncertainty,

produced by these conflicting accounts. 'Squire Thomas Cheyney[1]—a citizen of Thornbury township—rode up to the forces
under Sullivan with intelligence that the main body of the
British army had crossed the Brandywine, and was already at
hand, approaching from the north; and, being uncourteously
received by that General, demanded to be led to the Commander-in-Chief. This was done, and, although Washington
was at first disposed to doubt the correctness of the information, he was at length convinced of its truth, and immediately
disposed of his troops to meet the emergency. It is said that
some of the General's staff spoke rather sneeringly and in-
credulously of the rustic 'Squire's information, which roused
his temper. "If you doubt my word," said he to the Commander-in-Chief, "put me under guard until you can ask
ANTHONY WAYNE or PERSIE FRAZER[2] if I am a man to be be-

[1] Thomas Cheyney was a revolutionary patriot whose devotion to his country
was untiring—the very beau-ideal of an honest Pennsylvania Whig. While
the British army was in this section of country, he was ever on the alert, and
by keeping their movements in view, he materially aided Washington by imparting to him the information thus acquired. He possessed an unusual share
of sound discriminating common sense, and was widely known as a shrewd,
intelligent citizen and upright magistrate. He served as a Justice of the Peace
before, during and after the war; and portions of his dockets, which still exist,
show that he caused many to be arrested for treason, and for carrying stores to
the British army whilst in Philadelphia. A man by the name of Pennell, hired
one Crosby for a bushel of salt, then an item of some value, to decoy Cheyney
into the hands of the British, which he failed to accomplish, and after the termination of the war, Pennell sued him for the price of the salt before the Squire
himself. It is not certainly known what his judgment was.

[2] Persifor Frazer, a citizen of Chester County, was Captain of a company in
the 4th Battalion or Regiment of Pennsylvania troops, organized early in 1776,
and composed largely of Chester County men. The campaign of 1776 was
passed by this regiment at or near the fortress of Ticonderoga, during which
Captain Frazer was promoted to the rank of Major. In the campaign of 1777,
he was with General Wayne at the Battle of Brandywine. Four days after the
battle, he and Major Harper, while reconnoitering, were captured by the British
and taken with them to Philadelphia, where they were closely confined in the
new prison. On the 17th of March, 1778, Major Frazer made his escape and re-
joined the army, gallantly performing his duty at the Battle of Monmouth on
the 28th of June, 1778. While in the hands of the British, he was commissioned by Congress Lieut.-Col. of the 5th Regiment.

Persifor Frazer was a patriot well fitted for "the times that tried men's souls,"

lieved;" and then turning to the General's Attendants, he indignantly exclaimed—"I would have you to know that I have this day's work as much at heart as e'er a *Blood* of you!"

I will not detain you on this occasion with the details of the battle which ensued—the far-famed battle of Brandy-wine. Suffice it to say, that, after a severe contest, which was participated in by the gallant Lafayette, the Americans were defeated with a loss of three hundred killed and six hundred wounded, while the loss of the British was reported at one hundred killed and four hundred wounded. Three or four hundred were taken prisoners, chiefly of the wounded.

A considerable part of the British army remained from the 11th to the morning of the 16th of September in the neighborhood of the field of battle, the chief portion lying encamped about Dilworthtown, and south of it, on the properties then of Charles Dilworth and George Brinton. Gen. Howe had his head-quarters at a house near by, belonging to Israel Gilpin, still standing, and now owned by Elias Baker. During this time they had a cattle-pen near Chads' Ford, where they collected and slaughtered large numbers of cattle and other animals and preserved them for the use of the army. Nearly all the live stock in the country for a considerable distance around was taken from the inhabitants. In some instances payment was made in British gold, but generally no compensation whatever was given. The day after the battle, a detachment of the army, under Major-General Grant, marched to Concord Meeting House, where it was joined on the 13th by Lord Cornwallis with some light infantry and British grenadiers. From this point they moved to Village Green, a short distance from Chester, and there encamped, leaving a detachment at Concord to guard the wounded left in the Meeting House, and sending another to Wilmington, where there were some wounded.

The Americans, after the battle, retreated towards Chester, where they arrived by different roads and at different times

whose memory is proudly and deservedly cherished by his descendants, among whom are those who have acquired distinction in the forum, eminence in the walks of science and a gallantry in the Field, every way worthy of their honored ancestor.

in the night. On the arrival of Washington at this place about midnight, he addressed a letter to Congress, giving them an account of the disaster. On the next day the army marched by way of Darby to Philadelphia, where it was joined by straggling parties. The main body was encamped near Germantown, where they were allowed two or three days to rest.

The question has been frequently mooted whether the fact that the British had divided their forces at the Battle of Brandywine should not have been discovered sooner than it was, and the disastrous defeat which took place have been prevented. I entertain the opinion, from a personal knowledge of the entire section of country near where the battle was fought, that there was somewhere the most inexcusable negligence in not having earlier definitely ascertained the movements of the British army. The fords of the Brandywine where they were at all likely to cross, were all comparatively near to the Americans, and were easily accessible ; the country, though rolling, was comparatively open ; the roads were substantially the same as now, and their movements could have been easily discovered in time to have enabled Gen. Washington to have disposed of his troops to the best advantage. The distance from Chads' Ford to Jefferis' Ford is but six miles, and to Trimble's Ford about seven and a-half miles. It is now known that small bodies of the British light troops crossed at Wistar's (now Sager's) Ford, and at Buffington's (now Shaw's) Ford— the latter on the east branch, just above the forks, and both between Chads' Ford and Jefferis' Ford—some time before the main body of the army crossed at Jefferis' Ford, and yet no information of these movements appears to have been communicated to the Commander-in-chief. Tradition says that the great American chieftain was so conscious of the oversight in not having sooner discovered the movements of Howe, that he ever manifested a dislike and unwillingness to converse on the strategy of that day.

It has been usual to attribute the loss of the Battle of Brandywine to this want of timely intelligence of the movements of the enemy ; but it is problematical whether the Americans could have been successful under any circumstances.

The British army was well appointed and well disciplined ; a large part of the American army was, at the time, comparatively untrained, and this superiority of the British over the Americans would probably have enabled them to gain the day, even if Gen. Washington had received timely notice of all their movements.

While, however, there was certainly negligence in not having sooner discovered the disposition of the British forces, yet we must be gentle with the memories of those who served their country in the war of the revolution. It was a period far too trying to judge men as on ordinary occasions. The Americans were fighting not for fame or power, but for justice and liberty. They had left their homes and occupations to fight the finest troops of the most powerful nation of the world. When we consider the circumstances by which the patriots were surrounded, pitted against a foreign foe, and with a relentless and treacherous enemy at home, calling themselves loyalists, but better known by the designation of tories, our only wonder is, that success could attend their efforts ; and, looking at all the surroundings and the difficulties encountered and overcome, the disasters which befell the American arms became victories from the first gun which was fired in the struggle until the British laid down their arms at Yorktown.

The British steadily pursued their purpose to seize Philadelphia, and occupy it as their quarters during the ensuing winter.

As it was deemed important to save that city from falling into their hands, Washington resolved to risk another engagement ; for, although the Battle of Brandywine had resulted unfavorably to the American army, it was considered that the British had there gained little more than the battle-field, and the ardor of the troops was unabated.

At that time one of the principal crossing places of the Schuylkill was at Swedes' Ford, near the present southern limits of Bridgeport and Norristown, and as the British could not well cross lower down on account of the depth of the water, it was expected they would make the attempt to force a passage at that point, or higher up the stream.

On the 15th of September, Washington left his camp at Germantown, and with the main body of his army crossed the Schuylkill and marched up the Lancaster road, with the intention of meeting the enemy and again giving battle. He proceeded to a point near the junction of the Lancaster and Swedes' Ford Road, in East Whiteland Township, northwest of the Admiral Warren Tavern, and encamped his forces between that point and the White Horse Tavern, having his head-quarters at the residence of Joseph Malin, now belonging to Benjamin Carruthers.

The British commander, having received intelligence that Washington was advancing upon the Lancaster Road, resolved to attack him. The portion of his army which had been encamped in the neighborhood of Village Green—then known as the "Seven Stars"—left that point, under the command of Cornwallis, on the 16th of September, and proceeded northward towards the Great Valley, by what is known as the Chester Road, by way of the present villages of Glen Riddle, Lima, and Howellville, and by Rocky Hill and Goshen Friends' Meeting House.

On the morning of the 16th, Washington received information that the enemy were approaching by the way of Goshen Meeting House, and were already in the neighborhood of that place.

The two armies moved to positions between the White Horse and Goshen Meeting House, on the high ground south of the valley, and both commanders commenced making preparations for action. Some detachments were made by the Americans to reinforce the advanced guard, and keep the enemy in check until the army should be properly arrayed. To Gen. Wayne was assigned the duty of leading the advance and opening the battle. Skirmishing began between the advance of the forces under Wayne and the Light Infantry at the head of Lord Cornwallis' column, and a sanguinary battle would probably have been fought, but a rain-storm of great violence stopped its progress. A consultation was had as to whether the British should be received on the ground then occupied by our troops, or whether they should retire beyond the Great Valley, which was in the rear, and in which the ground was said to be wet,

and where, in case of a defeat, the artillery would certainly be
lost. Washington accordingly, after consultation, gave the order
to move, and the American forces retired and formed on the
high ground in the Great Valley, east of the White Horse and
north of the old Lancaster Road, and there remained until
about four o'clock in the afternoon awaiting the advance of the
British army.

Col. Timothy Pickering, Adjutant General of the American
army, gives the following account of these movements of the
army :

"On the 11th of September, 1777, the battle of Brandywine
took place. After carrying General Washington's orders to a
general officer at Chadsford, I repaired to the right, where the
battle commenced ; and remained by the general's side to its
termination at the close of the day. Orders were given for the
troops to rendezvous at Chester, whence they marched the
next day to the neighborhood of Philadelphia. When re-
freshed, and supplied with ammunition, the army again crossed
the Schuylkill river, and advanced to meet General Howe. On
the 16th of September, in the morning, information was received of the approach of the enemy. Some detachments
were made to reinforce the advanced guards, and keep the
enemy in check, until the American army should be arrayed
for action. General Washington ordered me to the right wing,
to aid in forming the order of battle. On my return to the
centre, I found the line not formed. Seeing the commander-
in-chief with a number of officers about him, as in consultation, I pressed my horse up to learn the object. It was a
question whether we should receive the British on the ground
then occupied by our troops, or retire beyond a valley in their
rear, in which the ground was said to be wet, and impassable
with artillery, which, in case of a defeat, would of course be
lost ; excepting that with the left wing commanded by General Greene, through which there was a firm road. By this time,
the fire of the troops engaged appeared to be drawing near. At
this movement, the consultation yet continuing, I addressed
General Washington. 'Sir (said I), the advancing of the British
is manifest by the reports of the musketry. The order of

battle is not completed. If we are to fight the enemy on this ground, the troops ought to be immediately arranged. If we are to take the high grounds on the other side of the valley, we ought to march immediately, or the enemy may fall upon us in the midst of our movement.' 'Let us move'—was the General's answer. The movement took place. It had begun to rain. The British army halted. Ours formed on the high ground beyond the valley, and there remained during a very rainy day."

The point where the skirmishing took place was on the high ground about one mile and a-half north of Goshen Meeting House, and half a mile or more a little west of south of the old "Three Tuns Tavern," on the property then of Thomas Rees, now belonging to the heirs of John Parry, deceased, in the north-eastern part of East Goshen Township. Twelve American soldiers were killed in the conflict and buried there. A few were also wounded, and some prisoners were taken by the British.

The British forces which had remained encamped near the field of battle at Birmingham and Chads' Ford, at the same time that Cornwallis moved northward from the Seven Stars towards the Great Valley by the Chester road, proceeded under Knyphausen, by way of the Turk's Head, now West Chester, towards the same point, with the view of joining the forces under Cornwallis. A part of this division, under Brig. Gen. Matthews, proceeded from the Turk's Head[1] northward by the Reading road to the Indian King tavern. From thence they passed across the farm of David Dunwoody, then occupied partly by himself and partly by his son James Dunwoody, and encamped on the north-east part of it near the Ship road, and overlooking the Valley. It was raining heavily and they at once took measures to protect themselves from the inclemency of the weather. The Hessian line, under the command of Count Donop, took the road leading from the Turk's Head to

[1] As the British forces were passing the Turk's Head tavern on their way to join Cornwallis, they were fired upon by a scouting party of Americans and two of their number killed. They were immediately buried inside of the garden fence of the tavern, near the intersection of the Philadelphia road. The remains of these men were dug up in the summer of 1827, in excavating the cellar for the house now occupied by Pierce's drug store, on High street.

the Boot tavern, and from thence northward towards the Ship tavern. When they reached the south valley hill, on the farm of Daniel Meredith, now owned and occupied by his grand-son Isaac Meredith, and were near to his residence, they encountered a detachment of the Americans, and a spirited skirmish took place, in which a few were killed on both sides, and a considerable number wounded, and some prisoners were taken by the Hessians. The killed were buried near to the dwelling of Daniel Meredith, and the wounded taken to the house of Dan'l Thompson, a short distance north of Meredith's, which was used as a hospital. The house, now torn down, stood immediately in front of the site of the present new house on the Ship road, belonging to Rev. Samuel L. Tennis. This engagement, which was interrupted by the rain, took place about the same time as that with the forces of Cornwallis near the Three Tuns tavern, already referred to. The points are about three miles distant from each other. Bullets and other relics of the war have frequently since been found on the sites of both of these engagements.

The Americans left their position near the White Horse about four o'clock in the afternoon of the 16th, and retired northward to the Yellow Springs, about five miles distant, where they arrived in the night. The division of Wayne encamped on the farm of Christian Hench, now partly owned by Joseph J. Tustin. Mr. Hench was an ardent patriot and liberally supplied their wants so far as it was in his power. An inspection disclosing the alarming fact that the army was not in a condition to engage in a conflict in consequence of their ammunition having been greatly damaged by the rain, and that scarcely a musket in a regiment could be discharged, the march was continued the next day to Warwick Furnace, on the south branch of French creek, in the northern part of Chester county, where there was an ordnance depot and some stores for the use of the army, from whence a fresh supply of arms and ammunition was obtained.

The storm lasted some time, the division of the British army, under Cornwallis, being encamped during its continuance, along the South Valley Hill, south and west of the Three Tuns tavern; that portion of the division of Knyphausen, under Gen.

Matthews, on the farm of David Dunwoody, and the Hessian line under Count Donop, on the farm of John Bull, south of the present residence of George W. Jacobs. Other forces lay at the Boot tavern, and north of it.[1] The head-quarters of Gen. Howe were at the Boot tavern, then kept by John Bowen, and of Lord Cornwallis during a part of the time at the house of George Hoopes, now owned by his descendant George Hoopes, of West Chester, a short distance north of Goshen Meeting House, and afterwards at the house of Daniel Durborow, now owned by Francis S. Fiss, about one mile west of the Three Tuns, or what is now known as the King road. All these houses are still standing.

On the evening of the 17th, Cornwallis with his division advanced to the Old Lancaster road, in the Great Valley, and took post about two miles distant from Knyphausen. On the 18th, the division under Knyphausen advanced on the Ship road northward to the Lancaster road, and thence eastward to the White Horse, where they joined the forces under Cornwallis on the same day, and the entire army moved down the Lancaster and Swedes' Ford Road into Tredyffrin township, and encamped on the south side of the Swedes' Ford Road at the present village of Howellville, and between that and the Village of Centreville. Gen Howe, the Commander-in-Chief, had his head-quarters at the residence of Samuel Jones, now belonging to Franklin Latch, a short distance west of Centreville, and Lord Cornwallis, at that of Abel Reese, now late of Mrs. Reese, near the bridge at the crossing of the Swedes' Ford Road and ChesterValley railroad. The quarters of Gen.

[1] The British forces, during this storm, burned and destroyed large numbers of fence rails on the properties where they encamped and those adjoining. After the close of the war, returns were made to the County Commissioners, in pursuance of an Act of Assembly, passed September 21, 1782, of damages and losses sustained from the troops and adherents of the King of Great Britain during the war, from which we learn that David Dunwoody reported among other things the loss of 8500 rails, Daniel Thompson, 8800; Thomas Lewis, 8000; Thomas Rees, 9000; John Bowen, 9000; Thos. Harris, 2500, and many other considerable numbers. Samuel Jefferis who owned the property late of Samuel R. Kirk, near Kirkland Station, on the West Chester railroad, who made no report, lost about ten thousand rails, and his farm lay unfenced for many years thereafter.

Knyphausen were east of Gen. Howe's and of Generals Agnew and Grey near Howellville.

From French Creek Gen. Wayne, on the 17th, was detached with his division, amounting to about fifteen hundred men and four field pieces, to join Gen. Smallwood, who had command of the Maryland militia, and was then in the rear of the British army. Wayne was ordered to harass and annoy the enemy, and to seize every occasion which might offer to engage him with advantage, and to endeavor to cut off the baggage-train, and by this means to arrest his march towards the Schuylkill, until the Americans could cross the river higher up, and pass down on the east side and intercept the passage of the river by the British.

Gen. Wayne proceeded to the duty assigned him, and on the 18th of September encamped about three hundred yards a little north of east of this point on land now belonging to Hannah G. Griffith, and which was about four miles in the rear of the enemy, distant from any leading road, and securely concealed, as he believed, from the knowledge of Howe. He established his head-quarters at the house of a man named King, now of Robert Hutchinson, on the east side of what is now called the Sugartown Road, and a short distance south of the gate by which these grounds are entered from that road.[1]

On the 19th of September, Gen. Wayne watched the movements of the enemy as far as was practicable with the view of attacking them, should they attempt to move. On the morning of that day, on the enemy's beating the reveille, he ordered his troops under arms, and took up the line of march for their left flank, and proceeded to within half a mile of their encampment, but found they had not stirred, and lay too compact to admit of an attack with prudence. In a letter to the Commander-in-Chief, written at Paoli after 10 o'clock A. M., he stated that the enemy would probably attempt to move towards evening.[2] They did not move, however, but on the 20th he re-

---

[1] Wayne was no doubt specially chosen for this service, as his home was in the neighborhood, and he was well acquainted with the locality.

[2] From the Life of Wayne, published in the "Casket," it appears that a num-

ceived what he believed was reliable information that the British commander would take up his line of march for the Schuylkill at 2 o'clock on the following morning, and he sent Col. Chambers as a guide to Gen. Smallwood, then near the White Horse, to conduct him to the place of encampment. When the junction with his forces should be effected, it was his design to advance upon the British rear and attack it while in the operation of moving. He had already reconnoitered a road leading along their right flank, and had determined on his plan of operation. To be in readiness for this purpose, he directed his men to lie on their arms, and, as it was raining, to protect their cartridge boxes with their coats, and that no time might be lost after the

ber of letters passed between Washington and Wayne on the 17th, 18th, and 19th of Sept. The following, however, are all I have met with:—

PAOLI, half after 7 o'clock A. M., 19th Sept.

DEAR GENERAL—

On the enemy's beating the reveille I ordered the troops under arms, and began our march for their left flank, but when we arrived within half a mile of their encampment found they had not stirred, but lay too compact to admit of an attack with prudence. Indeed their supineness answers every purpose of giving you time to get up—if they attempt to move I shall attack them at all events. This moment Capt. Jones of Bland's Dragoons brought in four prisoners; three of them belong to the Queen's Rangers and one artillery-man; they don't seem to know much about the movements of the enemy, nor the loss they sustained at Brandywine, but have heard it was very great.

There never was, nor never will be, a finer opportunity of giving the enemy a fatal blow than the present—for God's sake push on as fast as possible. Interim I am your Excellency's most obedient, &c.

PAOLI, ¾ after 10 A. M., 19th Sept.

DEAR GENERAL—

The enemy are very quiet, washing and cooking. They will probably attempt to move towards evening. I expect General Maxwell on the left flank every moment, and as I lay on their right, we only want you in their rear to complete Mr. Howe's business. I believe he knows nothing of my situation, as I have taken every precaution to prevent any intelligence getting to him—at the same time keeping a watchful eye on his front, flanks, and rear. I have not heard from you since last night.

I am your Excellency's most obedient, humble servant,

ANTHONY WAYNE.

READING FURNACE, 6 o'clock P. M. (Sept. 19).

DEAR SIR—

I have this instant received yours of half past three o'clock A. M. Having written to you already to move forward upon the enemy, I have but little to add.

arrival of Gen. Smallwood, he had his own horse brought out, saddled and holstered ready for mounting, and his cloak thrown over his horse to preserve his accoutrements from injury from the inclemency of the weather.

He had carefully guarded himself against surprise, planted pickets and sentinels, and thrown forward patrols upon the roads leading to the enemy's camp. Between nine and ten o'clock he received a visit from a friendly citizen of the neighborhood— a Mr. Jones—who had come to his quarters to give information, that a servant of Mr. Clayton, who had been taken by the enemy and afterwards liberated, had said that he had overheard some of the British soldiers speaking of an attack to be made upon Wayne's detachment during the course of the night. Gen. Wayne thought proper, in consequence, to take some additional precautions. He despatched a number of videttes, with orders to patrol all the roads leading to Howe's camp. He planted new pickets, one on a by-path leading from the Warren Tavern to the camp, and others to the right and in the rear. In addition to these, a horse picket was well advanced upon the Swedes' Ford Road. And having taken these precautions, he lay in momentary expectation of Gen. Smallwood's arrival, to enable him to take the offensive.

Although the British commander did not know where the forces under Gen. Wayne lay, there were *Tories* residing in the neighborhood who did, and by these he was informed of the precise locality and of the nature of the approaches to it. He at once sent Gen. Grey to surprise and cut him off, a service of a dangerous character, as 'Wayne's corps was known for its stubborn and desperate conduct in fight. Col. Musgrave, with

Generals Maxwell and Potter are ordered to do the same, being at Potts' Forge. I could wish you and those generals to act in conjunction, to make your advance more formidable; but I would not have *too much time* delayed on *this* account. I shall follow as speedily as possible with jaded men—some may probably go off immediately, if I find they are in a condition for it. The horses almost all out on the patrol. Cartridges have been ordered for you. Give me the earliest information of everything interesting, and of your moves, that I may know how to govern mine by them. The *cutting off* of the enemy's baggage would be a great matter.

Yours sincerely,
GEO. WASHINGTON.

the 40th and 55th Regiments were moved up to the Lancaster
road near the Paoli tavern, to be in a position to aid Gen. Grey,
if necessary, and to intercept any attempt by Wayne's forces to
retreat over that route. The watchword of the Americans for
that night was "Here we are and there they go," and this, the
tradition of the neighborhood says, through some treachery,
was communicated to the enemy.

Gen. Grey, guided by his Tory aids,[1] as is generally believed,
marched from his encampment near Howellville, up the
Swedes' Ford Road, and massed his troops on that road, as
near the camp of Wayne as possible, without betraying a
knowledge of his approach. From there he moved on up the
road to what is now known as the Valley Store, at the crossing
of the Swedes' Ford and Long Ford Roads, north of the Admiral Warren. At this point there was an American picket,
who fired and escaped. Tradition says the British made use
of the American watchword, but the picket discovered they
were not Americans, and fired. Gen. Grey then proceeded
south on the Long Ford Road to near the Admiral Warren,
where they encountered another picket, who also fired and escaped; from there he cautiously moved through the woods and
up the ravine through the south valley hill north of this point,
and near to the present Malvern Station on the Pennsylvania
Railroad.

The first intelligence Gen. Wayne received of the enemy's
advance was from one of the videttes whom he had sent out in
consequence of the notice received from Mr. Jones. Several

---

1 The Admiral Warren tavern was at that time kept by one Peter Mather, and
tradition has always charged him with having been active in piloting Gen.
Grey on the night of the massacre. His sympathy was doubtless with the British, but there is reason to question the truth of the tradition. He denied it
himself, and his daughter at the age of eighty years stated to a friend, that she
was eight years of age at the time, that her father was at home on that night,
that the British in their march to surprise Wayne came to the house and urged
her father to pilot them, but that he positively refused and did not go, and she
added, that it was a dreadful night to them. As somewhat corroborative of
this, it may be stated that several letters of British officers concerning the surprise, speak of having compelled a blacksmith residing close to the Warren
tavern to give them information and to accompany them, but make no mention
of Mather.

pickets had been silently bayonetted in the darkness, and being
missed by the patrolling officer, his suspicions were aroused,
and he hastened to the head-quarters of his commander with
the information. The troops were immediately ordered under
arms, and many of them were awakened from their slumbers
by the cry, " Up, men, the British are on you!" The night was
dark, and being rendered more obscure by the surrounding
woodland, much had to be left to conjecture as to the point of
attack. Having ascertained, however, that the enemy were advancing upon his right, where the artillery was placed, Wayne
directed Col. Humpton, his second in command, to wheel the
division by sub-platoons to the right, and to march off by the
left, and gain the road leading on the summit of the hill towards
the White Horse, being the road on which the division had
marched two miles the previous evening. The division wheeled
accordingly, and the artillery moved off; but owing to some
misapprehension, as is alleged, on the part of Col. Humpton,
the troops did not move, although they were wheeled and faced
for the purpose, until the second and third order had been issued. In addition to this, only part of the force took the right
direction, while the other part took a wrong one, and were
brought within the light of their fires, and thus gave the enemy
an advantage which should have been most assiduously guarded against. Gen. Wayne took the light infantry and first regiment, and formed them on the right, with a view to receive the
enemy and cover the retreat of the artillery.

Gen. Grey,[1] whose forces consisted of two regiments, the 42d
and 44th, the second battalion of light infantry, and the second
and tenth dragoons, was enabled, in consequence of the darkness and aided by the knowledge of his tory guides, to approach

[1] Winthrop Sargent in his life of Major John André, states that André was
an aid to Grey at Paoli. He had been appointed on his staff early in the summer of 1777, and was with him at the Battle of Brandywine, but on that occasion Grey's brigade, which formed part of the column of Cornwallis, was not
called into action. Its character was so high, that it was preserved intact as a
recourse in case Knyphausen failed. Major André had been a prisoner of war
on parole from November, 1775 until January, 1777, spending his time at Lancaster, Carlisle, and Reading, and during this period had frequently travelled
the Lancaster road, and was therefore doubtless of service to Grey on the night
in question.

very closely without observation. He gained Wayne's left about one o'clock in the morning. The troops under Wayne met the enemy with spirit, and gave them several close and well-directed fires, which did considerable execution. They were, however, soon obliged to give way before the superior numbers of the assailants. Seeing this, Gen. Wayne immediately flew to the fourth regiment, with which he again received the shock of the enemy's charge, and covered the retreat of the rest of his line. After being again compelled to retire, he rallied such of Col. Humpton's troops as had taken the proper course in their retreat, about three hundred yards in the rear of the last stand, where they were again formed ready to renew the conflict. Both parties, however, drew off without further contest, and Wayne retreated to the White Horse, carrying with him his artillery and ammunition, except eight wagons loaded with baggage and stores, which, with a considerable amount of arms, were left upon the field, and fell into the hands of the enemy.

The British forces amounted to nearly double the number commanded by Wayne. Gen. Howe had received from disaffected persons such accurate accounts of the strength and position of the American forces, as enabled him to give to his own detachment so decided a superiority as to insure victory. He knew from his guides the precise point where to make the attack, and was enabled to move with decision and accuracy, while Wayne was under the necessity of acting, in a great measure, from conjecture.

The British attack was made with bayonets and light horsemen's swords only, in a most ferocious and merciless spirit. In emulation of a remarkable action which took place in the German war, Grey ordered his men to remove the flints from their guns, that not a single shot should be fired, and thus gained the sobriquet of the "No-flint General." An officer of the British Light Infantry, in describing the attack, writes that, as they approached the camp of the Americans, General Grey "came to the head of the battalion, and cried out, 'Dash on, light infantry!' and, without saying a word, the whole battalion dashed into the woods; and, guided by the straggling fire of the picket, that was followed close up, we entered the camp and gave such a cheer as made the wood echo. The enemy were completely surprised; some with arms, others without, running in all directions in the greatest confusion. The light infantry bayonetted every man they came up with. The camp was immediately set on fire, and this, with the cries of the wounded, formed altogether one of the most dreadful scenes I ever beheld." Another officer of the light infantry, in writing to a friend, said: "Then followed a dreadful scene of havoc. The light dragoons came on, sword in hand; the shrieks, groans, shouting, imprecations, deprecations, the clashing of swords and bayonets, etc. etc.; no firing from us, and little from them, except now and then a few, as I said before, scattering shots, was more expressive of horror than all the thunder of artillery, etc., on the day of action.'" Even the wounded and sick were not spared, and many were killed after resistance on their part had ceased. It is this feature in the conduct of the British commander which has stigmatized it as " British barbarity " and " cold-blooded cruelty," and has given to this affair the title of the Paoli Massacre.

When the attack commenced, Gen. Smallwood, with about eleven hundred and fifty Maryland militia, and Col. Gist, with seven hundred men, were within a short distance of Wayne, whom they were hastening to join. Had they commanded soldiers of sufficient firmness, their sudden arrival might have greatly embarassed the British general, and even given a different turn to the affair. The raw militia commanded by them became, however, excessively alarmed, and could not be brought to face the enemy thus unexpectedly encountered, and the advance having fallen in with a small part of the enemy who were returning from the pursuit, they fled in confusion, with the loss of one man only, and Gen. Smallwood, with the

---

[1] In Lossing's Field Book of the Revolution, vol. 2, p. 161, 2d ed., N. Y., 1860, the following is given: A Hessian sergeant, boasting of the exploits of that night, exclaimed—" What a running about barefoot, and half clothed, and in the light of their own fires! These showed us where to chase them, while they could not see us. We killed three hundred of the rebels with the bayonet. I stuck them myself like so many pigs, one after another, until the blood ran out of the touch-hole of my musket."

remainder of his *Romans*, agreeably to the orders of Wayne, joined him at the White Horse.[1]

The loss of the Americans was about one hundred and fifty killed and wounded. The British reported their loss as eight killed, but the opinion of the neighborhood at the time was strongly against the veracity of this report, as many litters were seen to pass that night toward the British camp, and it is well known that they manifested extreme jealousy with regard to the discovery of the extent to which they suffered.[2]

The next morning the scene of the conflict was visited by the people of the neighborhood, one of whom was Joseph Cox, and the sufferings of the wounded were alleviated as far as circumstances would permit. It had rained heavily the night before, and to assuage their thirst, the water was dipped up with leaves and with the broad brims of their hats, from the pools which had formed, and given to the men. Fifty-three mangled dead were found upon the field, and decently interred by the farmers in one grave, immediately adjoining the scene of action, on the spot marked by yonder monument. While they were engaged in the act of burying the dead, a number of British

[1] *Copy of a Memorandum in the Handwriting of Capt. Thomas Buchanan, of First Pennsylvania Regiment.*

At the affair of the Paoli, in the fall of 1777, I was sent forward to Gen. Smallwood, that lay at the White Horse, to get him to cover our retreat and fix a place of rendezvous, &c. He sent me forward to try to stop as many of his broken troops that had taken the road to Downingtown. On coming near to there, I found where some of his artillery had thrown a field-piece into a limekiln, and had broke the carriage. I went on to Downingtown, and fixed a guard on the road to stop the runaways; got a wheeler and blacksmith to mend the carriage, and went down and put the cannon on the carriage, &c.

[2] Lieut. Samuel Brady, of Buffalo Valley, now in Union County, Pa., belonged to Capt. John Doyle's company of Independent Rifles, then attached to the 6th Pa. in Wayne's Brigade, and was with him at Paoli. Brady was on guard and laid down with his blanket buckled around him. The British were nearly on them before the sentinel fired. Brady ran, and as he jumped a fence, a soldier struck at him with a musket and pinned his blanket to a rail. He tore the blanket and dashed on. A horseman overtook him and ordered him to stop. He wheeled and shot the horseman dead and got into a small swamp, supposing no one in but himself. In the morning he found fifty-five men in it, of whom he took command and conducted to camp.— *From John B. Linn's Annals of Buffalo Valley, Pennsylvania.*

officers rode up and viewed the grounds, but did not interfere
with them. About two weeks thereafter, the body of another
dead soldier was found in the woods and buried where it lay.

Among those killed was Major Marien Lamar, of (now) Centre county, who fell in the midst of the British in the retreat.
His last words were, "Halt, boys, give these assassins one
fire!" He was instantly cut down by the enemy. In honor
of this martyr in the cause of his country, a township in Centre county erected in 1817, was given his name. Dr. Christian
Reinick, of Lancaster, Surgeon Mate of the 1st Pennsylvania,
was also killed.[1]

The unfortunate affair soon became the subject of animad-
version in the army, instigated, it was said, by those who were
envious of Wayne's rising reputation, and in consequence he
at once requested an inquiry into his conduct. This request
was granted, and soon after the Battle of Germantown a court-
martial was convened. The charge, which was preferred by
Col. Humpton, was, that Gen. Wayne "had timely notice of
the enemy's intention to attack the troops under his command
on the night of the 20th of September, and notwithstanding

_____

[1] Dr. R. C. Smedley, born and reared in the neighborhood, relates the following
traditions: "On the night of the massacre, while the slaughter was going on,
the family of Joseph Cox, living near by, on the property now owned by Wm.
G. Cox, on the State road, were aroused by a man outside calling to them. The
Battle of Brandywine having occurred but a short time before, and the family
knowing that soldiers were in the neighborhood, had been living in a state of
apprehension and excitement and were easily awakened. Joseph immediately
arose, hoisted the window and asked, "who is there?" "For God's sake get
up, we're all routed," replied the man, "don't you hear them?" At this every
member of the family was soon at the windows listening to the work of car-
nage. There was borne to them distinctly on that midnight air, the sounds of
the British as they rushed through the camp, in their demon-like madness and
murderous intent, crying out with vociferous yell the Americans' watchword of
that night, "Here we are and there they go," the cracking of leaves and bushes
as men rushed through them, and the groans of the wounded as they were
stabbed with swords and bayonets, becoming fainter and fainter until they died.

"Early the next morning, a soldier came to the house of Joseph Cox to bor-
row of him a plain coat and hat to wear back to the place to look after his fallen
comrades, saying he was afraid to go in his uniform, lest some of the English
might be lying around to kill any American soldiers that might return."

During the conflict, a soldier ran to a fence and tumbled over it and before
he could get up, the bayonets came crashing against the fence. He however
escaped. .

that intelligence, he neglected making a disposition until it was
too late either to annoy the enemy or make a retreat, without
the utmost danger and confusion." Gen. Wayne made a written answer to this charge against him, and, after a full investigation, the Court unanimously acquitted him of the charge, and
further declared that he had done everything that could be expected from an active, brave, and vigilant officer, under the orders which he then had, and they further added : "The Court
do acquit him with the highest honor."[1]

The attack upon Wayne's forces and their consequent retreat
frustated the contemplated operations against the right wing
and rear of the enemy, and enabled Howe to move without
being molested. On the morning of the 21st of September he
resumed his march, and in pursuance of his purpose to reach
Philadelphia, moved down the road leading to Swedes' Ford,
intending to cross the Schuylkill at that point : but there were
breastworks on the opposite side of the river, occupied by troops
placed there by Washington, and seeing this, he turned up the
river on the west side, with the intention of making its passage
at some of the fords higher up.

The American army under Washington, in order if possible
to prevent the British from passing the river, had in the mean
time moved from Warwick Furnace, and crossed the Schuylkill
at what was then known as Parker's Ford, at or near the present village of Lawrenceville, in this county—the officers and
men wading the stream, which was breast-high—and marched
southward on the east side, by way of the Trappe, as far as
the Perkiomen.

The British commander then made a feint of moving his
army northward along the west bank of the Schuylkill, with
the view of inducing the Americans to suppose that it was his
intention to gain their right, or else by a sudden movement to
seize the ammunition and other military stores deposited at
Reading. Washington, deceived by this movement, returned
up the eastern side of the river to the neighborhood of Potts-
grove, and while he was there, Gen. Howe, on the 23d of Sep-

[1] See "Papers relating to the Massacre," for a full account of this inquiry into the conduct of Gen. Wayne and his defence.

tember, suddenly wheeled his army, marched rapidly down the
river, and dividing his forces, crossed with little opposition at
Gordon's Ford, now Phœnixville, and at Fatland Ford, a short
distance below Valley Forge, and proceeded by easy marches
to Philadelphia, which he entered in triumph on the 26th of
September.

One of the great difficulties with which the American cause
had to contend, during the entire period of the Revolutionary
War. after the early enthusiasm had in some measure subsided
and war became a stern reality, was the fact that a portion of
the people were either apathetic or disposed to favor the British interest.

The region bordering on the Schuylkill River, through which
the armies passed, was largely disaffected towards the American cause, and for that reason Washington could procure very
little reliable information of the movements of the enemy.
Could he have obtained correct intelligence, he might have
foiled Howe and saved Philadelphia. We perhaps appreciate
too little the difficulties under which Washington sometimes
labored in obtaining correct information, by reason of this disposition among a portion of the people to withhold their aid
from the struggling cause.

The British army, in its march from the Head of Elk to
Philadelphia, occupied about two weeks in its passage through
Chester County, having entered it on the 9th of September,
1777, and left it on the 23d of the same month. It traversed
nearly the whole length of the southern part of the county
(then comprising within its limits the present county of Delaware), and also made incursions into several townships not on
the line of the main route, before making its exit in the
neighborhood of the present town of Phœnixville and of Valley Forge, and taking up its winter quarters in the quiet city
of Penn. This was the only time during the entire contest
that the soil of our good county was pressed by the foot of
the invader, if we except the occasional foraging expeditions
sent out from Philadelphia while it was occupied by the
British army.

The plunder and devastation perpetrated by the enemy—
English as well as Hessians—on the private property of pas-

sive non-combatants during this period, in violation of the
proclamation issued by Howe, was enormous and wanton,
while compensation for any portion of the property taken was
rarely made by those in command. Many families were stripped
of everything they possessed, and left in a state of perfect des-
titution. "The British army had not before passed through a
district of country so rich in agricultural productions, nor one
in which every farm-house was so well stored with everything
that could minister to the real comforts of life." Hence they
did not fail to gather a rich harvest, carrying off horses, cattle,
sheep, swine, grain, provisions, clothing, merchandize in stores,
liquors in public houses, and whatever they could lay their
hands on that could be used in the camp or on the march.
Independent, however, of the property thus carried off, the
wanton destruction of furniture and other articles which they
could not use was unworthy of the most barbarous people, and
this devastation was not confined to the track of the army, but
extended for a considerable distance on either side.[1]

For forty years the spot where the patriot dead of this field
lay interred was unmarked, save by a heap of stones; but on
the 20th of September, 1817, the Republican Artillerists of
Chester County, aided by their fellow citizens, erected a monument over their remains, appropriately inscribed. On that occasion an address was delivered by Major Isaac D. Barnard,
and an account of the massacre was given by the Rev. David
Jones, then in his eighty-second year, who had been the Chaplain to the ill-fated warriors, and who was on the ground on
that fatal night and barely escaped. The occasion was also
honored by the presence of Col. Isaac Wayne, the son of Gen.
Wayne.

Soon thereafter these grounds, containing twenty-three acres,
were purchased by the military organizations of Chester and
Delaware Counties, and set apart as a parade ground. On each

[1]While the British army lay in Tredyffrin township, a detachment was sent to
Valley Forge and destroyed property belonging to Col. William Dewees, valued
by him at £4,171, Pennsylvania currency, equal to over $11,000. Among the
property destroyed and taken from him was a Forge, Saw Mill, two large stone
dwelling houses, two coal houses and four hundred loads of coal, and twenty-
two hundred bushels of wheat and rye in sheaf.

returning anniversary of the massacre, for many years, the citizens, soldiers of these counties, and occasional visiting companies from Philadelphia and elsewhere, met here to participate in the ceremonies of the day, which, I believe, were for some years invariably closed with a sham battle. These visits were interrupted by the war of the Rebellion, but since its close, they have been resumed. The scene of this conflict is probably the best preserved of any that marked the progress of the Revolutionary War.

Sixty years have, in the progress of time, been added to the forty which preceded them, and on this one hundredth anniversary of the day on which the heroes there interred, laid down their lives that we might live free and independent, we meet to dedicate with loving hands a new and more stately and enduring monument to their memory.

It gives me pleasure to add, in conclusion, that while on the occasion of the dedication of the former monument, the assembly then present rejoiced in the presence of a son of Gen. Wayne, we to-day are honored, in the person of our first Vice-President, Capt. William Wayne, with a great-grandson of Chester County's brave and gallant hero, a gentleman who, inheriting the military qualities of his noble ancestor, was himself an officer in the Union Army during the late war with the South.

PAPERS RELATING TO THE PAOLI MASSACRE.

The following Account is from the Diary of Lieutenant afterwards Gen. Hunter, in the Historical Record of the 52d Regiment, and is printed in the Historical Magazine, col. 4, p. 346. N. Y. 1860.

As soon as it was dark, the whole battalion got under arms. Major-General Grey then came up to the battalion, and told Major Maitland, who commanded, that the battalion was going on a night expedition to try and surprise a camp, and that, if any men were loaded, they must immediately draw their pieces. The major said the whole of the battalion was always loaded, and that, if he would only allow them to remain so, he, the major, would be answerable that they did not fire a shot. The general then said if he could place that dependence on the battalion, they should remain loaded, but firing might be attended with serious consequences. We remained loaded, and marched at eight in the evening to surprise Gen. Wayne's camp. We did not meet a patrol or vidette of the enemy until within a mile or two of the camp, where our advanced guard was challenged by two videttes. They challenged twice, fired, and galloped off at full speed. A little further on there was a blacksmith's forge ; a party was immediately sent to bring the blacksmith, and he informed us that the picket was only a few hundred yards up the road. He was ordered to conduct us to the camp, and we had not marched a quarter of a mile when the picket challenged, fired a volley, and retreated. General Grey then came to the head of the battalion and cried out—Dash on, light infantry ! and, without saying a word, the whole battalion dashed into the wood, and guided by the straggling fire of the picket, that was followed close up, we entered the camp and gave such a cheer as made the wood echo. The enemy were completely surprised ; some with arms, others without, running in all directions in the greatest confusion. The light infantry bayonetted every man they came up with. The camp was immediately set on fire, and this, with the cries of the wounded, formed altogether one of the most dreadful scenes I ever beheld. Every man that fired was instantly put to death. Captain Wolfe was killed, and I received a shot in my right hand soon after we entered the camp. I saw the fellow present at me, and was running up to him when he fired. He was immediately killed. The enemy were pursued for two miles. I kept up until I grew faint from loss of blood, and was obliged to sit down. Wayne's Brigade was to have marched at once in the morning to attack our battalion while crossing the Schuylkill River, and we surprised them at twelve. Four hundred and sixty of the enemy were counted the next morning lying dead, and not one shot was fired by us, all was done with the bayonet. We had only twenty killed and wounded.

Account by an Officer of the second battalion, British Light Infantry. From an unsigned letter in the Materials for History, edited by Frank Moore, N. Y. 1861.

I have been in a more bloody affair at midnight on the 20th of September. The battalion I served in (the second light infantry), supported by three regiments and some dragoons, surprised a camp of the rebels consisting of 1,500 men, and bayonetted (we hear) from four to five hundred.

The affair was admirably conceived and executed. I will (as it is remarkable) particularize. I was released from picket at sunset—the preceding sunset I mounted—and was waked at nine at night to go on the bloody business. The men were ordered to unload ; on no account to fire. We took a circuit in dead silence ; about one in the morning fell in with a rebel vidette (a vidette is a horse sentinel), was challenged three times and fired. He was pursued but escaped. Soon after two foot sentries challenged and fired ; these escaped also. We then marched on briskly, still silent ; our company was advanced immediately preceding a company of riflemen, who always are in front. A picket fired upon us at the distance of fifteen yards, miraculously without effect. This unfortunate guard was instantly dispatched by the riflemen's swords. We marched on through a thick wood, and received a smart fire from another unfortunate picket—as the first, instantly massacred. We then saw the wigwams or huts partly by the almost extinguished light of the fires and partly by the glimmer of a few stars, and the frightened wretches endeavoring to form. We then charged. For two miles we drove them, now and then firing scatteringly from

behind fences, trees, &c. The flashes of the pieces had a fine effect in the night.
Then followed a dreadful scene of havoc. The light dragoons came on sword
in hand. The shrieks, groans, shouting, imprecations, deprecations, the clashing of swords and bayonets, &c., &c.; no firing from us and little from them,
except now and then a few, as I said before, scattering shots, was more expressive of horror than all the thunder of the artillery, &c., on the day of action.

From the Diary of the Revolution, by Frank Moore, vol. 1, page 498. Copied
from Gaine's Mercury.

Sept. 22.   Yesterday the British having received intelligence of the situation
of General Wayne, and his design of attacking their rear should they attempt
to pass the Schuylkill, a plan was concerted for surprising him, and the execution intrusted to Major-General Grey. The troops for this service were the fortieth and fifty-fifth regiments under Lieutenant-Colonel Musgrave, and the second battalion of light infantry, the forty-second and forty-fourth regiments,
under the general. The last detachment marched at ten o'clock last night —the
other at eleven. No soldiers of either were suffered to load; they that could
not draw their pieces took out their flint. The general knew nearly the spot
where the rebel corps lay, but nothing of the disposition of their camp. He rep-
resented to the men that firing would discover them to the enemy, kill their own
friends, and cause a confusion favorable to the escape of the rebels, and perhaps,
productive of disgrace to the British. On the other hand, by not firing, they
would know the foe to be wherever fire appeared, and a charge insured his destruction; that amongst the enemy, those in the rear would direct their fire
against whoever fired in front, and consequently destroy each other.

General Grey marched by the road leading to the White Horse, and took
every inhabitant with him as he passed along. About three miles from camp
he turned to the left and proceeded to the Admiral Warren, where, having
forced intelligence from a blacksmith, he came in upon the out sentries, pickets,
and camp of the rebels. The sentries fired and ran off, to the number of four,
at different intervals; the picket was surprised, and most of them killed in endeavoring to retreat. On approaching the right of the camp, the line of fires
were perceived, and the light infantry, being ordered to form to the front, rushed
along the line, putting to the bayonet all they came up with, and, overtaking
the main herd of fugitives, stabbed great numbers, and pressed on their rear till
it was thought prudent to order them to desist. The forty-fourth regiment, advancing in line likewise, closed up in support of the light infantry, putting to
the sword such of the rebels as the heat of the pursuit had escaped that corps;
whilst the forty-second came on in a third line as a reserve. Upwards of two
hundred were killed and as many more wounded. Seventy-one prisoners were
brought off—forty of them being badly wounded were left at different houses
on the road. The British loss consisted of Captain Wolfe and one or two men
killed, Lieut. Hunter and five men wounded. It was about one o'clock this
morning when the attack was made, and the rebels were then assembling to
move toward the King's forces.

Extract from General Howe's Letter to Lord George Germain.
See Remembrancer, vol. 5, p. 413.

HEAD-QUARTERS, GERMANTOWN, Oct. 10, 1777.

MY LORD:—

* * * * * * * * *

The enemy crossed the Schuylkill on the 18th, above French Creek, and encamped upon the river on each side of Perkyomy Creek, having detached troops to all the fords of Schuylkill, with cannon at Swedesford and the fords below it.

Upon intelligence that General Wayne was lying in the woods with a corps of fifteen hundred men, and four pieces of cannon, about three miles distant, and in the rear of the left wing of the army, Major-General Grey was detached on the 20th, late at night, with the Second light-infantry, the Forty-second and Forty-fourth regiments, to surprise this corps.

The most effectual precaution being taken by the General to prevent his detachment from firing, he gained the enemy's left about one o'clock, and, having by the bayonet only, forced their out-sentries and pickets, he rushed in upon their encampment, directed by the light of their fires, killed and wounded not less than three hundred on the spot, taking between seventy and eighty prisoners, including several officers, the greater part of their arms, and eight wagons loaded with baggage and stores. Upon the first alarm the cannon were carried off, and the darkness of the night, only, saved the remainder of the corps. One captain of light-infantry and three men were killed in the attack, and four men wounded. Gallantry in the troops, and good conduct in the General, were fully manifested upon this critical service.

* * * * * *

With most perfect respect,
I have the honor to be, &c.,
W. HOWE.

Letter of Col. Samuel Hay to Col., afterwards Gen., William Irvine.

CAMP AT THE TRAP, Sept. 29, 1777.

DEAR COLONEL: Since I had the pleasure of seeing you the division under the command of General Wayne has been surprised by the enemy with considerable loss. We were ordered by his Excellency to march from the Yellow Springs down to where the enemy lay near the Admiral Warren, there to annoy their rear. We marched early on the 17th instant, and got below the Paoli that night; on the next day fixed on a place for our camp. We lay the 18th and 19th undisturbed, but on the 20th at 12 o'clock at night the enemy marched out, and so unguarded was our camp that they were amongst us before we either formed in any manner for our safety, or attempted to retreat, notwithstanding the General had full intelligence of their designs two hours before they came out. I will inform you in a few words of what happened. The annals of the age cannot produce such a scene of butchery—all was confusion—the enemy amongst us, and your regiment the most exposed as the enemy came on the right wing. The 1st Regiment (which always takes the right) was taken off and posted in a strip of woods, stood only one fire and retreated, then we were next the enemy, and as we were amongst our fires they had a great advantage of us. I need not go on to give the particulars, but the enemy rushed on with fixed bayonets and made the use of them they intended. So you may figure to yourself what followed. The party lost 300 privates in killed, wounded, and missing besides commissioned and non-commissioned officers; our loss is Col. Grier, Captain Wilson, and Lieutenant Irvine[1] wounded (but none of them dangerously), and 61 non-commissioned and privates killed and wounded, which was just half the men we had on the ground fit for duty. The 22d I went to the ground to see the wounded, the scene was shocking—the poor men groaning under their wounds, which were all by stabs of bayonets and cuts of light horsemen's swords. Col. Grier is wounded in the side by a bayonet, superficially slanting to the breast bone. Capt. Wilson stabbed in the side, but not dangerous, as it did not take the guts or belly; he got also a bad stroke on the head with the cock nail of the lock of a musket. Andrew Irvine was run through the fleshy part of the thigh with a bayonet. They are all laying near David Jones' tavern. I left Capt. McDowell with them to dress and take care of them, and they are all in a fair way of recovery. Major LaMar, of the 3d Regiment, was killed and some other inferior officers. The enemy also lost Captain Wolfe killed, and four or five light horsemen, and about 20 privates, besides a number wounded. The general officers have been in council for three days, and the plan is fixed, but what it is we do not yet know. Inclosed you have the state of the British army with their loss at Brandywine; you have it as I have it, and may judge of it as you think proper.

You will see by this imperfect scrawl how many sorts of ink I have written with—all borrowed, and the inkstands dry, as I have no baggage, nor have had any these four weeks, more than one shirt and one pair of stockings, besides what is on my back; the other officers are in the same way, and most of the officers belonging to the division have lost their baggage at Colonel Frazer's, taken by the enemy. I have nothing new to inform you of. My compliments to Mrs. Irvine and Mrs. Armstrong; let her know the General is very well, and lodges near our camp.

I am with great respect,

Yours affectionately,

SAMUEL HAY.

P. S.—The officers of the division have protested against Gen. Wayne's conduct, and lodged a complaint and requested a court martial, which his Excellency has promised they shall have. This has brought down his pride a little already.—*Historical Magazine*, N. Y., 1859, p. 349.

GEN. CHARLES GREY.

Gen. Charles Grey, the British officer who "conducted" the massacre at Paoli, also distinguished himself subsequently in superintending the bayoneting of sixty-nine unarmed men of Baylor's regiment, near Tappan, N. Y., to whom he ordered *no quarters to be given*, although they begged for their lives on

---

[1] Captain Andrew Irvine received seventeen bayonet wounds in all, one of which penetrated through his company-book, which, in the confusion, he had taken up and thrust into the breast-pocket of his coat to carry off. He never entirely recovered, but died soon after the close of the war from the effects of these wounds.

bended knees. After these *heroic* achievements, he returned to England, where he was dubbed by King George III—presumably as a reward for his *meritorious services*—*Sir* Charles Grey, *Knight of the Bath*. He was created Baron Grey of Howick in 1801, and in 1806, Viscount Howick and Earl Grey. One of his sons became Prime Minister in 1830, and others of his descendants have been conspicuous in British annals.

PAPERS RELATING TO THE TRIAL OF GEN. WAYNE.

From Hazard's Register of Pennsylvania, vol. 3, p. 372.

REQUEST OF GEN. WAYNE FOR COURT MARTIAL.

Shortly after the 20th of September Gen. Wayne addressed the following letter to Washington:

SIR: I feel myself very much injured until such time as you will be kind enough to indulge me with an inquiry into my conduct concerning the action of the 20th of September.

Conscious of having done my duty, I dare my accusers to a fair and candid hearing; dark and insidious friends I dread, but from an open and avowed enemy I have nothing to fear. I have no other mode of showing them forth to open view than through your means. I must, therefore, beg an immediate investigation by a court martial. Your compliance will much oblige your Excellency's most obedient humble servant, ANTHONY WAYNE.

From Saffell's Records of the Revolution.

ORDER OF GEN. WASHINGTON TO COURT OF INQUIRY.

HEAD-QUARTERS, TOAMENSING, Oct. 11, 1777.

The Court of Inquiry, of which Lord Sterling is President,[1] now sitting at the President's quarters, is to inquire into the conduct of Brigadier-General Wayne, viz., that he had timely notice of the enemy's intention to attack the troops under his command on the night of the 20th ult.; and, notwithstanding that intelligence, he neglected making a disposition until it was too late either to annoy the enemy or make a retreat without the utmost danger and confusion. The President will give notice when the Court can enter on the inquiry, and when the parties and evidence are to attend. GEORGE WASHINGTON.

COURT MARTIAL CONVENED.

A general court martial, of which General Sullivan was President, was held the 25th, 26th, 27th, and 30th of October, for the trial of Brigadier-General Wayne, on the following charges, *viz:*—

That he had timely notice of the enemy's intention to attack the troops under his command, on the night of the 20th of Sept. last, and, notwithstanding that intelligence, neglected making a disposition until it was too late either to annoy the enemy or make a retreat without the utmost danger and confusion.

---

1 It consisted of Genls. McDougall and Knox, Cols. Spencer and Clark.

DEFENCE OF GEN. WAYNE.

After the expiration of five weeks, during which period the tongue of slander has not been idle, I am happy to bring my case before a court of whose honor and impartial judgment I cannot have the least doubt. I shall not intrude on the patience of this court by any useless preface, but proceed to answer the charge.

The first part of the charge exhibited against me, that "I had timely notice of the enemy's intention to attack the troops under my command," is very readily answered.

I shall briefly notice what these gentlemen call a *timely notice*. A Mr. Jones, an old gentleman living near where we were encamped, came to my quarters between nine and ten o'clock at night, and informed me before Colonels Hartley, Broadhead and Temple, that a servant boy belonging to Mr. Clayton had been taken by the enemy and liberated again, who said that he had heard some of their soldiers say that they intended to attack me that night. Although this could not be deemed a *sufficient notice* upon any military principle, yet I immediately ordered out a number of videttes in addition to those already planted, with directions to patrol *all* the roads leading to the enemy's camp. I also planted two new piquets, the one in front on a blind path leading from the Warren to my camp, the other to the right, and in the rear, which made on that night not less than six different piquets. I had, exclusive of these, a horse piquet under Captain Stoddard, well advanced on the Swedes' Ford Road, being the very way the enemy marched that night. But the very first intelligence which I received of their advancing was from one of the videttes which I sent out in consequence of the *timely notice* from Mr. Jones, who had only *time* to go about a mile before he met the enemy. Immediately on his return the troops were all ordered to form, having been warned to lay on their arms in the evening, for a purpose which I shall presently mention. At this time it was raining, and in order to save the cartridges from wet, I ordered the soldiers to put their cartouch-boxes under their coats. This, gentlemen, does not look like a surprise, it rather proves that we were prepared either to move off or act as the case might require, when once apprized which way the enemy were actually advancing. To have made any move previously to ascertaining that fact, might have been attended by fatal consequences, totally subversive of the views of the Commander-in-Chief. So soon as it was discovered that the enemy were pushing for our right, where our artillery was planted, Major Ryan carried my orders to Col. Humpton and to the division to wheel by sub-platoons to the right, and to march off by the left, and gain the road leading on the summit of the hill towards the White Horse, it being the very road on which the division moved the previous evening. The division wheeled accordingly, the artillery moved off, but, owing to some neglect or misapprehension, which is not uncommon in Col. Humpton, the troops did not move until a second and third order were sent, although they were wheeled and faced for the purpose. At the very time this order for the retreat was at first given, and which I presumed was obeyed, I took the light infantry and the first regiment, and formed them on the right, and remained there with them and the horse, in order to cover the retreat. If this was not *making a disposition*, I acknowledge I know not what a disposition is.

Those troops met and received the enemy with a spirit becoming free Americans, but were forced to give way to numbers. The neglect or misapprehension of Col. Humpton had detained the division too long, otherwise the disposition would have been perfect. I was, in consequence, necessitated to form the fourth regiment to receive the enemy and favor the retreat of the others; this Col. Butler and the officers of the infantry of that regiment were concerned in and witness of. About three hundred yards in rear of that I again rallied such of the divisions as took the proper route; those who went a contrary way and out of supporting distance, perhaps Col. Humpton can give the best account of. Here I have a fair and ample field for recrimination were I so disposed. I shall waive the subject, and beg leave to read the orders which I received from time to time from his Excellency, Gen. Washington.

In the eyes of gentlemen and officers I trust that I stand justified for the part I took on that night. I had the fullest and clearest advice that the enemy would march that morning at two o'clock for the river Schuylkill, and, in consequence of this intelligence, I had reconnoitered a road leading immediately along the right flank of the enemy, with Cols. Humpton and Hartly, and had the men *lying* on their arms, to move (as soon as Gen. Smallwood should arrive,) not *from* but *to* the enemy. For this purpose I had sent Col. Chambers as a guide, to conduct that officer into my rear, who, with his division was expected to arrive every moment, from two in the afternoon until we were attacked, at which time he was within a short distance of our rear, and retreated to the White Horse.

I shall just put a serious question or two, and then submit the matter to the decision of this court. Suppose that, after all these repeated orders from his Excellency, and the arrival of Gen. Smallwood, I had retreated before I knew whether the enemy intended to attack me or not, and that they should have marched for the Schuylkill that morning, which they actually did, would not these very gentlemen have been the first to default me for putting it out of my power to attack their rear? Would not his Excellency, with the greatest justice, have ordered me in arrest for cowardice and disobediency of his repeated peremptory and most pointed orders? Would not I have stood culpable in the eyes of the world? Would I not justly have merited immediate death or cashiering? I certainly would. What line could I follow but the one I trod? What more could be done on the occasion than what was done? The artillery, ammunition, etc., were covered and saved by a body of troops who were rallied and remained on the ground more than an hour after that gentleman, Col. Humpton, the prosecutor, had effected his escape from *danger*, although, perhaps, not without *confusion*.

I hold it needless to say any more, or to take up the time of this court on the occasion. I rest my honor and character, which to me are more dear than life, in the hands of gentlemen who, when deciding on my honor, will not forget their own.

DECISION OF THE COURT.

The Court, having fully considered the charge against Brigadier-General Wayne, and the evidence produced to them, are *unanimously* of opinion that Gen. Wayne is not guilty of the charge exhibited against him, but that he on the night of the 20th ultimo did everything that could be expected from an *active, brave,* and *vigilant* officer, under the orders which he then had. The Court do acquit him with the highest honor.

The Commander-in-Chief approves the sentence.

The Evidence of Capt. James Wilson, of the First Pennsylvania Regiment. See Historical Magazine, vol. 3, p. 375, N. Y. 1859.

That on the night of the 20th Sept[r], Genl. Wayne Personally placed me With the Light Infantry, his orders to me Was, Stand like a Brave Soldier and Give them fire. his Orders I Obey'd as Long as Possible, but the Enimy being too numerous forsd me to Give Way to the middle Fence, Where I Rallied about Thirty men and Gave them the Last Fire.

JA. WILSON,
Capt 1st Regt.

(On the back, in the handwriting of Lord Stirling, are the following questions and answers:--)

Q. "What distance was the Light Infantry advanced from ye right of ye Division when you received the enemy?"

A. "300 yards."

Q. "How long was ye placed to oppose the Enemy before they came to you at Firing distance?"

A. "About 8 minutes, & then not above a rod distance."

SKETCH OF COL. RICHARD HUMPTON.

Col. Richard Humpton, who is understood to have preferred the charge against Gen. Wayne for his conduct at the "affair of the Paoli," was a native of Yorkshire, England, where he was born in 1733. He was for some time a Captain in the British army, when he resigned his commission and emigrated to Pennsylvania. When the revolutionary contest came on, a commission in the Continental army was offered to him which he accepted. He was a brave man and stood high in the esteem of Gen. Washington, by whom he was frequently entrusted with important and responsible duties, and was employed by him confidentially on various occasions. At the Battle of Brandywine, where he had a command, his horse was shot under him, when he coolly ungirthed the saddle, slung it over his shoulder and proceeded to place it on another horse. At the Battle of Germantown he had the command of a Brigade, which was in action. After the revolution, he settled on a farm in Chester county, where he resided the remainder of his life. He received the appointment of Adjutant General of Pennsylvania from Governor Mifflin, with whom and his Secretary Alexander J. Dallas, Dr. Benjamin Rush, and other distinguished worthies of his day, he was on intimate terms. He was one of the original members of the Society of the Cincinnati, and his name occurs in the list of members between those of two gallant Pennsylvanians, Gen. Anthony Wayne and Gen. William Irvine. He died in December, 1804, leaving no descendants, and was interred in the burying ground of Friends' Meeting at Caln.

From Lewis' Letters on the History of Chester County.

APPEARANCE OF GEN. WAYNE.

Gen. Wayne was about the middle size, with a fine ruddy countenance, commanding port and eagle eye. His looks corresponded well with his character, indicating a soul noble, ardent and daring. At this time he was about thirty-two years of age, a period of life which perhaps as much as any other, blends the graces of youth with the majesty of manhood. In his intercourse with his officers and men, he was affable and agreeable and had the art of communicating to their bosoms, the gallant and chivalrous spirit which glowed in his own.

ORATION BY HON. WAYNE MAC VEAGH.

Fellow Citizens :

This place looks to-day much as it looked a hundred years ago. About it there are more highways and wider, larger tracts of cultivated land and better tilled, more dwellings and barns and more spacious, but all else is unchanged ; and the prospect it offers us is now, as it was then, very quiet and unpretending. As far as the vision can range, there is no sign of gleaming river or high mountain or great city, no sign even of man at work in mine or manufactory, or otherwise than as a simple tiller of the ground.

Few prospects, however, can be fuller of contentment and peace than the landscape which surrounded us upon every side as we journeyed hither, the fertile plains so lately reaped and yet sown with the seed of another harvest, the more fertile valleys, the broad pastures with their browsing herds, the graceful swell of the distant hills tolerant of culture to the top, or crowned with the exquisite beauty of woodlands just beginning to array themselves in the glory of autumnal color, and above all the happy homes of men and women intelligent enough to know their duty and brave enough to do it. From a part, the whole may be judged, and such, in general outline, is the county of Chester.

This county is as old as the province, and, therefore, far older than the state of Pennsylvania. It first received William Penn upon its soil, and great numbers of its citizens have always been his followers. Their exalted precepts of religion

and piety, and their faithful illustration of those precepts in use-
ful, honest, and virtuous lives are known and honored of all
men.   They were, however, conscientiously opposed to war,
and upon that great day when at Concord bridge

> "The embattled farmers stood,
> And fired the shot heard round the world,"

it is certain that many of the citizens of this county were opposed to strife in any form, and it is probable that many others
shared the mistaken belief of zealous and patriotic John Dick-
inson, that "two hundred years of happiness and present prosperity resulting from English laws and the union with Great
Britain, demonstrated that America could be wisely governed
by the King and Parliament."   In view of the prevalence of
this opinion, and of the peaceful principles of so large a proportion of the people of Chester County, it is a source of gratification to us, her children, that she sent so many gallant soldiers
to the field, and through the whole conflict kept so high the spirit
of her patriotism.   Whenever since the Revolution she has heard
the summons of her country to battle, she has fitly answered it.
The last answer was in our own hearing, and we know that it was
without distinction of creed.   In truth, great numbers of her
sons in every struggle in which the country has been engaged,
have "climbed the fiery ridges of battle," and gained, not only
for themselves, but also for her, their cherishing mother, imper-
ishable renown for valor in war as well as for virtue in peace.
It is, therefore, as becoming as it is wise that we should assemble upon this spot, consecrated by the blood of so many of the
patriots of the Revolution, upon this centennial anniversary of
their sacrifice, in order that we may contemplate anew their
virtues and the greatness of our obligations to them, and thus
attain a truer appreciation of the blessings of the free government they founded.

Contemplation of the men and the events of that critical
period in history cannot fail to exert an elevating influence upon ourselves.   It removes us from the narrowing cares of our
daily lives.   It lifts us above the unsatisfactory standards of public duty with which we vainly try to content ourselves.   It
brings us into the higher and purer air of the patriotism of the

Revolution. It sets us face to face with men who were possessed by the early American spirit in its best estate, its self-
reliance, its fearlessness in investigation, its thoroughness of
conviction, its practical good sense, its vivid conception of
its own relation to the forces at work in the world, its high
aims, its undaunted courage, its unquestioning faith in God and
liberty, its profound hold upon the future, and its noble capacity for sacrifice in a good cause. In such communion a sordid
and selfish public spirit, with low methods to mean ends, tends
to disappear, and a cowardly and corrupt public life becomes
less possible. Indeed, as we stand in the presence of the men
and the events of the Revolution, despondency gives place to faith,
and the memorable words instinctively recur to us with which
Mr. Burke closed the noblest of orations : " If we are conscious of our situation, and glow with zeal to fill our places as
becomes our station and ourselves, we ought to auspicate all
our public proceedings on America with the old warning of the
church, *Sursum Corda*. We ought to elevate our minds to the
greatness of that trust to which the order of Providence has
called us. By adverting to the dignity of this high calling, our
ancestors have turned a savage wilderness into a glorious em-
pire, and have made the most extensive, and the only honorable
conquests, not by destroying but by promoting the wealth, the
number, and the happiness of the human race." ·

In these centennial days we cannot, therefore, hope to discover a better method of acquiring a high and pure sense of
public duty than by comtemplating the conduct and character
of the men who pledged " their lives, their fortunes, and their
sacred honor " to that cause, whose cost they had calmly counted, and whose immeasurable consequences to the welfare of
mankind they not imperfectly apprehended. They well knew
that the American Revolution was not an accidental occurrence.
They well knew that it was not caused by the taxing of tea or
the attempt to compel the use of stamped paper. They well
knew that the real causes of the struggle and its true inspiration
were far older and far deeper, as old as the struggle for liberty,
as deep as the aspiration of man for advancement. They
well knew that there was a providential order in the education

of the world, and that the great steady lines of a divine purpose
were visible everywhere in human history, as each people, in
the fulness of time, made its alloted contribution to the progress of the race. Their minds were indeed happily "elevated
to the greatness of their trust." James Otis had declared that
"the world was at the eve of the highest scene of earthly power and grandeur that had yet been displayed to the view of
mankind; who would win the prize," he said, "was with God;
but human nature must and would be rescued from the general slavery that had so long triumphed over the species."
John Adams had declared that "a grand scene and design in
Providence" was opening "for the illumination of the ignorant,
and the emancipation of the slavish part of mankind all over
the earth."

The simple truth is that the leaders of the war of independence, whether in the forum or in the field, stood upon a mount
of observation, whence they were permitted to see something
of the greatness of the opportunity delivered into their hands,
something of the possible influences of their sacrifices upon the
future history of the world, and to realize that their words were
but "echoes of the eternal voice," themselves but instruments
of the "infinite will," their great battle for freedom but part of
"the essential movement of the world;" and this was "their
happy and divine fortune."

We are assembled to-day to honor their memories by restor-
ing with greater solidity of structure and in greater beauty of
design, the monument erected sixty years ago in commemora-
tion of the brave little band of patriots who were attacked and
defeated here by a much larger body of British troops, upon
the night of the twentieth day of September, 1777. Indeed, it
is not permitted to us, as citizens of Chester County, to celebrate with thanksgiving any victory of the Revolution, or to re-
count with exultation any triumph of the continental army.
Where we stand, occurred the massacre of Paoli. Near us, on
the one hand, are the hills of Brandywine, and on the other
the hills of Valley Forge. These three are the only historical
scenes of the war of the Revolution within the borders of the
county of Chester; and the only memories we are able to as-

sociate with them are the memories of a great battle lost, of a
grave disaster sustained, and of awful and prolonged sufferings
endured.

There is, however, one memory imperishably associated with
the battle lost at Brandywine, with the brave men slaughtered
at Paoli, with the frightful winter at Valley Forge, which Chester County may always cherish with pride and joy. It is the
memory of Anthony Wayne.

The career of this extraordinary man is full of interest and of
instruction; and it ought to be gratefully and proudly remembered, not only by the county of Chester, but also by the com-
monwealth of Pennsylvania in which he was born, lived, and is
buried. He came of good, stalwart, English ancestry, resident
for many generations in Yorkshire, followers in religion of Mar-
tin Luther, and in politics of John Hampden and Oliver Cromwell. In the latter part of the reign of Charles II. Anthony
Wayne, the elder, removed to the county Wicklow, in Ireland,
and was engaged in farming in that country when James II.
was expelled, and William of Orange ascended the English
throne. Two years thereafter occurred the battle of the Boyne,
and upon that scene of the old struggle between tyranny and
freedom in church and state, the grandfather of the hero of
Stony Point commanded a company of dragoons in the service
of King William, and fought stoutly and well for the protestant
religion and the liberties of Englishmen. For thirty years longer he braved the perils and endured the privations common to
all "the hated Englishry within the pale;" but when he was
sixty years of age, instead of looking only for his final place of rest,
he gathered his household together, took counsel of his faith
and his courage, and sought a new home in the new world.
He seems to have been eminently worthy of membership in
that goodly company of adventurous spirits, the early American
colonists, who were still living under the influence of the spirit-
ual and intellectual renaissance of the sixteenth and seven-
teenth centuries, controlled by a profound moral consciousness,
partly the effect of the Reformation, and enlightened by an im-
agination vivid and fearless, partly the effect of the splendid
outburst of genius in thought and action, which, "in the stately

procession of historic periods " will always distinguish the age of Elizabeth.

Anthony Wayne, the elder, arrived at Philadelphia in 1722, and in 1724 selected a home for himself and his family in the neighboring township of Easttown, in this county, about three miles from this place, where he passed the remainder of his days. His son, Isaac Wayne, seemed to inherit in large degree the strong mind, the strong will, and the liberal principles of his father ; and he was always prompt to answer every call of public duty, whether as a member of the provincial legislature, or as an officer in Indian warfare. He continued to live where his father had settled the family, and there, on the first day of January, 1745, was born to him a boy, to be named with the name of the trooper of the Boyne, and destined so to wear it as to keep it fresh forever in the memory of his countrymen.

Of the early life of General Wayne we know but little, and it is not important that we should know more. We do know that he displayed at a very early age his military disposition, for his tendency as a boy to indulge in the mimicry of war does not rest upon the traditions usual in the case of great captains. It is attested by a letter of his uncle, a school-master, in whose charge he had been placed, who wrote to his father : " One thing I am certain of, Anthony will never make a scholar. *He may make a soldier.* He has already distracted the brains of two-thirds of the boys under my charge by rehearsals of battles and sieges," and in place of the usual amusements "he has the boys employed in throwing up redoubts and skirmishing."

One of these predictions was not verified by the event, for he made such substantial progress in his studies that when he left the academy at Philadelphia, at the age of eighteen, he had acquired sufficient knowledge of the different branches of a liberal education to enable him to associate with educated men upon terms of perfect equality, and to take a leading part in affairs of business and of state with credit and distinction. He was given by nature an attractive personal presence, and his manners were excellent and dignified.

He thus entered upon life with many and important advantages, and before he had completed his twenty-first year he was

selected, upon the special recommendation of Benjamin Franklin, as the agent of a company of merchants of Philadelphia to
superintend the settlement of Nova Scotia. This enterprise
engaged his time and attention for several years. He then returned to the family home and quietly lived there, never losing
sight, however, of those great issues between the colonies and
the mother country which were growing in importance day by
day. At school, as agent of the Nova Scotia Company, and as
a farmer, were passed the first thirty years of his life. They
were uneventful years, or eventful only as they gave form to his
character, and prepared him for the work which was before him.

The summons to the second and greater period of his life
found him not only a willing but an ardent patriot. He was a
member of the assembly of deputies of the province which
met in the spring of 1774 to consider its condition, its prospects,
and its duty. He was a member of the convention which assembled in the fall of 1774, whose proceedings encouraged the
friends of resistance in all the other colonies. He was a member of the provincial legislature which met in the winter of the
same year, and was distinguished in that body for his out-
spoken advocacy of the rights of America. He was a member
of the committee of safety constituted in the summer of 1775,
for the purpose of putting the province in condition for military
service. In the early autumn of that year his mind had reached
a definite conclusion that the controversy had passed from the
arbitrament of argument to that of the sword, and he, therefore,
devoted his time and attention to acquiring and imparting a
knowledge of military tactics, and thus in some measure pre-
paring himself and his compatriots for the trial of their forti-
tude which he clearly saw awaiting them.

On the third day of January, 1776, he was commissioned, by
authority of the continental Congress, then sitting at Philadelphia, colonel of the regiment he had raised and disciplined in
this county, and he was immediately ordered to join General
Lee at New York, and from that city he led his regiment to take
part in the unfortunate expedition in Canada, under the command of General Sullivan. He was not obliged to wait long
for his first experience of war, for at the battle of the Three

Rivers his regiment was not only actively engaged, but he was himself seriously wounded. The command, however, devolved upon him, and he was obliged to conduct the retreat which the failure of the attack rendered necessary. In this, his first engagement, he seems to have exhibited all the qualities which were destined to give to his military career such great distinction, absolute fearlessness in the presence of danger, excellence of judgment wholly undisturbed by the din of arms, and, above all, that great quality which he shared with all men possessed of military genius, confident expectation of victory.

For the seven years which followed the engagement at the Three Rivers, the story of the life of General Wayne is part of the history of the Revolution. Placed in command of the forces at Fort Ticonderoga by General Schuyler in the latter part of 1776, and promoted by congress to the rank of brigadier-general early in 1777, he was nevertheless restless at being inactive, and succeeded in May of that year in obtaining permission to join the main army in New Jersey, and thus share the hazards of the memorable campaign then just beginning.

Doubtless much of his anxiety for this transfer from the quiet of the fortress of Ticonderoga to the stirring adventures of the field, was due to his earnest temperament, which could ill endure the safety of repose while others were privileged to fight for the cause to which he had given himself with absolute devotion; but much of his desire for the transfer was also doubtless due to the fact that the change would bring him into immediate association with General Washington, and enable him to enjoy the advantages of his counsel and companionship. How it would have intensified General Wayne's desire to take part in the campaign of 1777, if he could have foreseen its fortunes and have known that more than once his fellow patriots would join issue with the foe upon the soil of his native county, and almost within sight of his home.

The commander-in-chief soon formed a high opinion of him, and in his report to congress of the twenty-second day of June, 1777, spoke of him in terms of high praise. Dr. Rush wrote to him: "I need not say that in the field we expect that the Pennsylvanians will show us 'the mettle of their pasture' in the day of trial. Let no other state bear away from us the

palm of military glory :" and General Wayne with equal pride
promptly answered, " You may rest assured that the Pennsylvanians will not give up 'the palm of military glory,' to any
troops on earth."

You have just listened with evident interest and appreciation
to the interesting story of the movements of the revolutionary
army from its entry into this county in that campaign, until its
withdrawal from it after the disaster at this place, and you have
heard how gallantly and judiciously General Wayne behaved
at Paoli. It will, therefore, be impossible hereafter to misun-
derstand or misrepresent the occurrences of the fatal night we
are met to commemorate, or to question the justice of the
unanimous judgment of the court martial, which received the
hearty approval of General Washington, that "on the night of the
twentieth day of September, 1777, General Wayne did everything
that could be expected from an active, brave, and vigilant officer,"
and that for his conduct on that occasion he is entitled "to the
highest honor."

In the battle of Germantown he again won the praise of General Washington, for his division fought not only bravely, but
also victoriously. In his letter to his wife he laments the loss
of his horse killed within a few yards of the enemy's front, and
mentions that he was slightly wounded in the left hand and
left foot, but he declares that notwithstanding the final repulse
"it was a glorious day, our men are in high spirits, and I am
confident we shall give them a total defeat the next action,
which is at no great distance." Alas! such expectation was
only the hope of a soldier always eager for battle, and between
the day at Germantown "and the next action" were to be expe-
rienced, through many weary months of winter, lack of clothing, lack of shelter, lack of food in the huts at Valley Forge.
During all that winter General Wayne was earnest and unre-
mitting in his endeavors to alleviate the sufferings of the troops
under his command, by urgent entreaties to Congress, by personal solicitations of his friends for aid, and by successful forays
within the enemy's lines for provisions.

In June, 1778, when it was known that the British troops
were about to evacuate Philadelphia, out of seventeen general
officers, General Wayne and General Cadwalader alone voted to

attack the enemy on the march, and a week later, when General
Cadwalader was absent, and the commander-in-chief asked the
question, "will it be advisable to hazard a general action?"
General Wayne alone gave his voice for battle.

His opinion was approved by General Washington, who resolved "to take his measures on his own responsibility." Accordingly he ordered General Wayne to join the advance, and
placed the movement which resulted in the battle of Monmouth,
under the command of General Lafayette, who had not opposed,
although he had not supported General Wayne's opinion, and
with them went Colonel Hamilton of the headquarters' staff.
The Marquis de Lafayette, Alexander Hamilton and Anthony
Wayne, riding together to battle over the plains of Monmouth
on that summer's day, is a picture always worthy of our contemplation with affection and with pride ; and that the part our
hero bore in the struggle was worthy of that high companionship is attested by the generous words of General Washington :
"The catalogue of those who distinguished themselves is too
long to permit of particularizing individuals ; *I cannot, however, forbear mentioning Brigadier General Wayne, whose good
conduct and bravery throughout the whole action deserves particu-
lar commendation.*" General Wayne's own exultation was reserved, as usual, for his native state. In his letter to his wife
he declared, "Pennsylvania showed the road to victory."

Like so many of his distinguished associates in the continental army, General Wayne was in its truest and best sense a
citizen-soldier ; and in the stirring vicissitudes of war, he never
abated his interest in political controversies. Whenever the
army was in winter quarters he sought the seat of government,
and endeavored to quicken the patriotism of the members of
the legislature, and to elevate their aims in their different sphere
of duty. Indeed, he continued always to interest himself in
the political affairs of this county, as well as of the state
and the nation : and his influence was always on the side of
a patriotic devotion to the best interests of the country. Such
devotion was apparently as far from being general then as now,
for General Washington, writing at that time to a friend, uses
words strangely applicable to-day : "People, in general," he
says, "seem to think that to make money, and to get places,

are the only things now remaining to be done; and it is a fact," he adds, " too notorious to be concealed that Congress is rent by party, and that much business of a trifling nature and personal concernment withdraws their attention from matters of great national moment."

An ardent soldier and a citizen of public spirit, General Wayne was also warmly attached to his family and his home. He was naturally of a domestic disposition and rural tastes ; and his letters are filled, not only with the tenderest affection, but with frequent allusions to the pleasures of the social intercourse and the "many little endearing amusements," as he calls them, of his life upon his farm. Writing to President Reed, he declares that his highest ambition is to be allowed to return to it, "with safety to my country and honor to myself."

He had been permitted to spend several months of the spring of 1779 in Philadelphia and in Easttown, but in the latter part of June, General Washington re-called him, by an urgent message, to the army ; and upon his arrival he discovered that the duty expected of him was the recapture of Stony Point. With the story of that great and historic achievement you are all familiar, as well as with the very considerable influence it exerted upon the future course of the war, by re-inspiring the despairing patriotism of the colonies, and by convincing both Great Britain and France that the liberties of America were really unconquerable. The excellence of the plan devised by General Wayne, and the accuracy and vigor of its execution proved him to possess military judgment of a high order as well as gallantry and energy. General Washington indeed wrote to Congress, " *He improved upon the plan recommended by me*, and executed it in a manner that does honor to his judgment and bravery." Congratulations poured upon him from every side. His compatriot in arms, Arthur St. Clair, wrote from the army, " It is an event that makes a great alteration in the situation of affairs, and must have important consequences. It is, in short, the completest surprise I ever heard of." His compatriot in politics, Benjamin Rush, wrote from Philadelphia : " Our streets for many days rang with nothing but the name of General Wayne. You are remembered continually next to our

9

great and good Washington. You have established the national character of our country." Charles Lee, whom he had once challenged to mortal combat, magnanimously wrote from his retirement in Virginia: "I can have no interest in paying my court to any individual. What I shall say, therefore, is dictated by the genuine feeling of my heart. I do most sincerely believe that your action at the assault of Stony Point is not only the most brilliant in my opinion through the whole course of the war, on either side, but that it is one of the most brilliant I am acquainted with in history." General Lafayette, who had temporarily returned to France, wrote from over the sea: "With the greatest pleasure I take this opportunity of congratulating you on your admirable expedition at Stony Point. I was particularly delighted at hearing that this glorious affair was conducted by my very good friend."

Thenceforward General Wayne was engaged in the usual duties of a general officer in the field, until the army went into winter quarters in New Jersey, when he visited Philadelphia again to endeavor to obtain some alleviation of the sufferings of his command. He was re-called by General Washington in June, 1780, and remained in active service during the comparatively uneventful campaign of that year; but during the fall and early winter the condition of the Pennsylvania troops filled his mind with the gravest apprehensions; and in the most urgent entreaties to Governor Reed, to Robert Morris, and to other gentlemen of position and influence, he besought them to provide against the misunderstanding existing as to the term of enlistment of many of the soldiers of this state, and the continuance of the terrible exposure and suffering of all of them. No adequate measures, however, were taken; and the grave troubles he apprehended culminated on the first day of January, 1781, in the mutiny of the Pennsylvania line. By his steadfast courage and his excellent judgment, aided by the respect and affection the soldiers entertained for him, he was able to avert the consequences of the revolt most dreaded; and he succeeded in June of the same year in joining General Lafayette in Virginia with a very respectable body of soldiers from this state.

He took an active part in all the operations against the army of Cornwallis, and in the subsequent siege of Yorktown. Soon after the surrender of that place he was ordered to move with his command to the assistance of General Greene in South Carolina, to whom he promptly reported and by whom he was as promptly assigned to the difficult task of "re-instating the authority of the Union within the limits of Georgia."

His duties in this expedition were political as well as military : for he was particularly instructed "to try by every means to soften the malignity and deadly resentments subsisting between whigs and tories." In six months he had driven all the British forces from the state, and had done much to inaugurate a feeling of mutual good will between its inhabitants; for like almost all great soldiers he was very magnanimous in his judgment, as well as in his treatment of the vanquished. In his own words he believed that it was "the interest of the United States as well as of Georgia to reclaim men who at another day would become valuable members of society ; to admit the repentant sinner to citizenship after a reasonable quarantine," and "to pass an act of oblivion of all offences committed during the war." Having secured peace to Georgia, he returned to the assistance of General Greene, then sorely pressed in South Carolina, and in December, 1782, he received the surrender of the city of Charleston in that state, and thus ended his active military services in the war of the Revolution.

The character of those services was promptly recognized by Congress in his promotion to the brevet rank of Major General the tenth day of October, 1783, and at the ensuing election Chester County honored herself by asking him to represent her in the general assembly of the state. He accepted her trust, and discharged its duties with the same capacity, zeal, and high sense of honor which had distinguished him in the field.

In addition to his own extensive estates in this county, which he had inherited from his father, the state of Georgia had given him a very considerable property in recognition of his services within her borders, and the greater portion of his time was necessarily devoted for several years to his private affairs. He consented, however, to act as a member of the convention in this state in 1787 to decide upon the propriety of the adoption of the constitution of the United States; and the people of Georgia in 1792 offered him a seat in Congress. This latter honor he declined, but he promptly accepted in the same year the high distinction offered him by President Washington, the place of commander in chief of the army of the United States.

The greatness of this honor can only be adequately appre- hended by considering the greatness of the responsibility at- taching to it at that time. For ten years the northwestern border had been the scene of Indian hostilities. For ten years the military forces of the nation had been unable to protect its own hardy frontiersmen, or to punish its savage foes; and the total defeat of the army under General St. Clair in November, 1791, had caused the country to despair of any successful issue of the war. General Washington was still in his first term as president, and certainly no greater burden was resting upon him than the duty of finding a happy solution of this grave difficulty. His admirable judgment of men was of inestimable service to him at this juncture. He knew that the army needed a leader of consummate wisdom—patient and calm—seeking by every honorable method to secure peace without fighting, but able and determined, if necessary, to secure peace by the sword. Such a leader General Washington believed General Wayne to be; and the event amply justified his judgment. General Wayne was literally obliged to create a new army, to enlist it, to discipline it, to give it confidence in itself and its weapons, and to accustom it to the evolutions necessary in savage warfare; and after more than two years spent in preparation, and in fruitless negotiations with the enemy, he attacked them, gained a glorious and decisive victory, and se- cured to the vast territory he had rescued the blessings of a permanent peace.

At last the warfare of his life was ended. From Canada to Florida, from almost within hearing of the sea at Monmouth to the Indian lodges on the Miami, he had been engaged in battle; and as he turned his face homewards he seemed to see a long vista of quiet days, "with honor and with troops of friends." It was ordered otherwise, and during his journey eastward, on the fifteenth day of December, 1796, he died at a

military post on the shores of Lake Erie, in the meridian of his
life and his glory.   Near the home where he was born and
lived, whither when absent his heart had always strayed to
keep company with wife and children, and where he hoped,
alas! how vainly, to pass many happy years of contemplation
and repose, is the beautiful churchyard of St. David's Church
at Radnor, and there, citizen of worthiest spirit, patriot pure in
heart, soldier without fear, Anthony Wayne rests in peace.

Men and women of Chester County: Let us resolve that we
will not wholly lose the benefit of his example.   Let us strive
to rise to a higher and truer appreciation of the privileges and
the duties of the inheritance of American citizenship.   The
principles of government for which our fathers fought is to be
found in the Declaration of Independence, proclaimed in peril
and sustained by sacrifices, and not in the old Constitution
framed in peace and by compromises of conflicting interests
and principles.   Those compromises inevitably contained the
seeds of the future antagonisms which steadily increased until
they overshadowed the whole land and threatened the existence
of the government.   The sacred duty was thus devolved upon
this generation of defending and maintaining American liberty
against the foes of its own household, and of securing, at an
awful cost in blood and treasure, the perpetuity of the American Union by incorporating the doctrine of the Declaration in
the very text of the Constitution, thereby making it an indis-
soluble part of the fundamental law.

The doctrine is that "all men are created free and equal,
and endowed by their Creator with certain inalienable rights,
among which are life, liberty, and the pursuit of happiness."
These words are plain and direct, easily understood, and need-
ing neither gloss nor commenting.   They express clearly and
fully the American principle.   They ought to be " written upon
the palms of our hands, and worn as a frontlet between our
eyes," to remind us continually that this government rests, as
upon a rock, upon the principle that every citizen is in legal
and political rights the equal of every other, entitled to precisely the same measure of protection for his " life and liberty,"
and to precisely the same measure of freedom of thought and
action in his " pursuit of happiness."

In order to secure stability and permanence to government
resting upon such a basis, its citizens must be worthy. They
must learn to be faithful to the American principle without
qualification or abatement. They must learn to recognize will-
ingly and cheerfully the supremacy of the laws they assist to
make. They must learn the inexorable limitations upon the
functions of government, where its capacity for beneficent action begins and where it ends. They must learn to prefer
their country to their party. They must learn to prefer unpal-
atable truth to palatable falsehood. They must learn to regard
every form of corruption in the public service as a hateful crime.
They must learn to labor earnestly and unceasingly to restore
to American statesmanship its ancient dignity, ability, and character, by purifying and elevating the purposes and the spirit of
our politics. They must learn to inculcate peace and good-will
between all sections and all classes, by taking care that every
class and every section enjoys the equal protection of the law.
Above all, they must learn the indispensable lesson, that if
America is to continue mighty and free, giving joy to her
children and hope to the world, it can only be because her citizens, in the words of John Milton, have been "instructed and
inured in the perpetual practice of truth and righteousness, and
casting far from them the rags of their old vices, have pressed
on hard to that high, and happy emulation, to be found the
soberest, wisest, and most Christian people."

These are the final moments of the memorial ceremonies of
this place and this day, and we are fitly employing them as our
best tribute to the fathers, by striving to apprehend the greatness of our opportunity and our duty as their descendants, by
striving to see, if only as in a vision, the beauty of true patriotism, the radiance and the blessing of a public life in America,
unstained and joyous and free. In such endeavors we are wholly
in sympathy with the heroism and the sacrifices of the Revolution, worthy of communion with its spirit, conscious of a new
ardor in our love of country, conscious of a higher standard of
public duty; and as we leave these honored graves, with our
souls awakened and elevated by the patriotic associations which
hallow them, our last words over them are words of reverent
prayer, that the dead who rest here, "shall not have died in
vain, that this nation shall, under God, have a new birth of freedom, and that government of the people, by the people, for the
people, shall not perish from the earth."

APPENDIX.

At a meeting of the "Republican Artillerists of Chester
county," held on the 4th of July, 1817—Major Isaac D. Barnard, presiding—after the proceedings in honor of the day were
concluded, the following preamble and resolutions were presented by Dr. William Darlington and unanimously adopted:

"On the 20th of September next, it will have been *forty years*
since a number of our revolutionary heroes, commanded by
the gallant GEN. WAYNE, were massacred in the most savage
manner by the British, in a night attack, near the *Paoli*. The
soil which has been consecrated by the remains of these patriots, is exposed to the invasion of every rude and careless
footstep, with no enclosure to protect it—without even the
humble memorial of a stone to designate the spot where sleep
our brave defenders. Yet a few short years, and conjecture
alone could point to the turf which wraps the men, who laid
down their lives that we might live free and independent.

Moved by sensibilities which these reflections call forth, and
which they can never wish to repress, the *Republican Artillerists* of Chester county believe it would be highly becoming
in them to attempt such measures as will enable them to pay
a tribute of respect, which has so long been due to the memory of departed merit. They, therefore,

Resolve, That Isaac D. Barnard, Joshua Evans, and Joseph
Pearce, Esquires, be a committee to make arrangements for
enclosing, in a durable manner, the graves of the brave men
who perished in the massacre, near the Paoli, on the 20th of

September, 1777 ; and also to procure a stone, with an appropriate inscription, to be placed in such part of the enclosure as shall be deemed most expedient.

Resolved, That it be enjoined upon said committee to confer with such of our surviving revolutionary patriots as can conveniently be consulted, with respect to the most eligible mode of performing this duty ; and also that the committee be directed to open a subscription paper for the purpose of defraying the expenses of the same, to which our fellow-citizens generally are hereby respectfully invited to contribute.

Resolved, That soon as the said committee shall be enabled to go on with the work, they be directed to have the same executed in the best possible manner ; and, if practicable, to have it in such a state of forwardness that it may be completed, in the presence of the company, on Saturday, the 20th of September next.

Resolved, That in case the undertaking can be accomplished by the time aforesaid, this company will assemble at the *Paoli*, on the anniversary of the catastrophe, and proceed from thence to the place of burial, to close the ceremony with the usual military honors."

The committee thus appointed made the following report at a meeting of the Republican Artillerists held at the Boot Tavern, on the 30th of August, 1817 :

"The committee appointed at the meeting of the Artillerists, on the 4th of July, 'to make arrangements for enclosing in a durable manner the graves of the brave men who perished in the massacre near the Paoli, on the 20th of September, 1777, and also to procure a stone, with an appropriate inscription, to be placed in such part of the enclosure as shall be deemed most expedient,' having engaged in the duties of their appointment, have now the satisfaction to acquaint the company with the successful result of their labors. Their first object was to secure the ground where the remains of our gallant countrymen are interred, for the purpose of erecting the contemplated works. This they happily accomplished. They then immediately proceeded to carry into full effect the laudable and patriotic intentions of the company. They accordingly consulted several of the surviving Revolutionary patriots, and having obtained their views on the subject, they personally examined the grounds to be enclosed, and have fixed upon the position, size, height and shape of the wall to be built. Workmen are now employed upon it who will have it finished in due time. The committee in further execution of their duty, and in accordance with the views of the venerable survivors of the Revolutionary war, have purchased a handsome marble monument to be raised within the enclosure. This is now in the hands of an architect, in the city of Philadelphia, who is engaged in cutting the inscription upon it. It will be completely lettered, finished and ready upon the grounds before the wall is entirely built. The whole work is in such a state of forwardness, that the committee feel themselves justified in saying that it will be completely ready for the performance of the funeral rites contemplated on the 20th of September next."

After which the following resolutions were read and unanimously adopted, viz:

Resolved, That this company will parade on Saturday, the 20th of September next, at 10 o'clock, A. M., at the Paoli, with their artillery prepared with twenty rounds of blank cartridges, to proceed from thence in procession at 11 o'clock precisely, to the place of interment, to perform, in connection with their military brethren, the military honors due on the occasion.

Resolved, That all the surviving officers and soldiers of the Revolution, in this and the adjacent counties, be and they are hereby particularly requested to attend and unite with the company in paying the last offices of respect to the memories of their unfortunate countrymen.

Resolved, That Isaac Wayne, Esq., and the Rev. David Jones, the former chaplain of Gen. Wayne's brigade, be and they are hereby particularly invited to favor the company with their presence on that day.

Resolved, That the general and commissioned officers of the First and Second Brigades of the Third Division, Pennsylvania Militia, be and they are hereby requested to attend in uniform, to join in the funeral procession.

Resolved, That the several volunteer corps in Chester and the adjacent counties, be and they are hereby requested to attend and participate with the company in performing the accustomed military honors.

Resolved, That the contributors to the monument, as well as our fellow-citizens generally, be also, and they are hereby respectfully requested to attend and unite with the military on that day.

Resolved, That Isaac D. Barnard, Wm. Darlington, and Jacob Neiler, be a committee to prepare a plan of the procession, confer with the commanding officers of the volunteer corps, and to make every full and necessary arrangement which the occasion calls for.

Resolved, That Isaac D. Barnard, Esq., be appointed to prepare and deliver an appropriate discourse upon the occasion.

The committee subsequently made the following additional report :

" The committee have the honor further to report that in conjunction with a few respectable citizens of the neighborhood, among whom they had the satisfaction to enumerate the venerable Gen. Brooke and Isaac Wayne, Esq., they proceeded to dig the foundation for the monument, and soon discovered that for the better security of the superstructure it would be advisable to disinter that portion of the relics of the patriotic soldiers which occupied the dimensions of the foundation. This melancholy task was executed with that veneration and solemnity which the occasion was so peculiarly calculated to inspire. The principal parts of the bones of four bodies were raised, and a repository being formed in the centre of the foundation, they were again carefully committed to the earth. The committee, as well as those associated with them on the occasion, derived great satisfaction from witnessing at the distance of forty years from the interment of these brave men, the very visible marks of attention which had been bestowed on their inhumation by a few of their worthy and patriotic fellow citizens in the midst of a barbarous enemy. The grave has been dug north and south, and the bodies regularly laid east and west. The hats, shoes, clothing and armor of the gallant, though unfortunate wearers, have been consigned to the grave with them. The committee, presuming that a specimen of each of these articles would not be an unacceptable presentment to those who have honored them with an appointment connected with the pious and patriotic act of a monumental notice of those departed heroes, have accordingly reserved a few of these specimens, which are subject to their orders.

Respectfully submitted, * "

The *tumulus* or cluster of graves in which the soldiers were interred, was enclosed with a substantial stone wall, forming a rectangle sixty-five feet long from north to south, by twenty feet wide, with a gate in the middle of the western side wall, and a marble monument, about nine feet in height, was erected in the centre of the enclosure, upon the four sides of the die of which were engraved the inscriptions given on pages five and six of this volume, and which were prepared by Dr. William Darlington.

The following order was then issued :

REPUBLICAN ARTILLERISTS, ATTENTION !

You will parade in complete uniform at the Paoli, on Saturday next, the 20th inst., precisely at 10 o'clock in the morning, in order to perform, in conjunction with your military brethren, the ceremonies contemplated at the completion of the monument in honor of Revolutionary patriotism.

By order, WM. DARLINGTON, O. S.

Sept. 15, 1817.

On the 20th of September the military and citizens convened at the Paoli Tavern, and at eleven o'clock a procession was organized by *Col. Cromwell Pearce*, late of the 16th Regiment, U. S. Infantry, who acted as officer of the day, and the line of march to the site of the monument was taken up in the following order :

Capt. Harris, Union Troop of Chester and Delaware, in advance.

Col. Cromwell Pearce, Officer of the Day.

Revolutionary Officers.

Isaac Wayne, Esq., and Rev. David Jones.

Officers of the U. S. Army and Navy.

Republican Artillerists of Chester County, Commanded by Major Barnard, (with an elegant brass field piece.)

Capt. Cooper's Junior Artillerists, from Philadelphia.

Capt. Wersler's Chester County Volunteer Light Infantry.

Capt. Holdgate's Montgomery Blues.

Capt. G. G. Leiper's Delaware Fencibles.

Brig. Gen. Wm. Brooke and staff, and officers of 3d Division, Penn'a Militia.

Field officers of Militia, from Philadelphia.

Capt. Holstein's troop of Cavalry, from Montgomery county.

Capt. Smith's Delaware County Troop.

Contributors and Citizens generally.

The column moved in this order up the Lancaster turnpike road as far as the Warren Tavern, where it wheeled to the left and proceeded by the Sugartown road to the site of the monument, which it approached with solemn music performed by the two bands attached to Capt. Harris' troop and the Republican Artillerists respectively, accompanied by the music of the other corps. By this circuitous route, about three miles in extent, the whole ground of the scene of action during the massacre was included. Having arrived at the monument, the troops and others took the several stations assigned to them, and an appropriate address was delivered by Major Isaac D. Barnard. The committee of superintendence then proceeded to put the last hand to their labors by adjusting the pyramid which crowns the monument. This was succeeded by an interesting account of the massacre by the Rev. David Jones, the former chaplain to those ill-fated warriors, who was on the ground at the time of that event. When he had finished his remarks, the ceremonies were concluded by twenty rounds from the field piece by the Republican Artillerists, and several vollies of musketry from the light troops. The procession was then resumed, and having retired some distance the several companies were dismissed, and the whole business of the day terminated in the most decorous and becoming manner.

The attendance evinced that the memory of the men of '76 was still cherished with a holy fervor, and that the spirit of those times was still emphatically the spirit of the American people. The numbers, brilliancy and respectability of the assemblage had probably then never been equalled on any occasion, in Chester county. Upwards of four hundred volunteer troops, of different descriptions, appeared completely equipped, and the concourse of citizens, as described by a writer of the day, was immense.

The Paoli Parade Ground contains twenty-two acres and three-quarters, and is held by two deeds of conveyance. The first was given by Col. Cromwell Pearce and wife, of East Whiteland township, Chester county. It is dated December 24, 1822, and granted and conveyed forever to Lieutenant Colonel William Darlington and Major Samuel Anderson, Commanding officers of the Chester and Delaware Battalions of Volunteers, a tract or piece of land situate in Willistown township in the said county of Chester, containing twenty-two acres and one hundred and ten perches of land, more or less, commonly known as the Paoli Parade Ground, " to have and to hold the said tract or piece of land with the appurtenances in Trust as a place of parade forever, for the use and benefit of all Volunteer Corps lawfully organized that have contributed towards the purchase of the same, or that may think proper to assemble together."

This piece of land did not contain the monument, and on September 20th, 1832, the lot on which the monument stands, containing ten perches of land, was ceded by John Griffith and wife to Colonel William Harris, Colonel Emmor Elton, John S.

Yocum and David Meconkey, Majors, field and commanding officers of the 1st Regiment of Chester and Delaware County Volunteers.

The Committee are indebted to the kindness of Theo. W. Bean, Esq., of Norristown, author of "Washington at Valley Forge One Hundred Years Ago, or the Foot Prints of the Revolution," for the use of the plate from which the accompanying map of East Penn'a, is printed. The map was prepared for Mr. Bean's work above referred to. A few additions have been made, with Mr. Bean's permission, to render it more illustrative of the historical discourse contained in this volume.

EAST PENN.ᴬ

www.ingramcontent.com/pod-product-compliance
Lightning Source LLC
Chambersburg PA
CBHW021522270326

41930CB00008B/1041